From your excerpts and your chapter headings this will be one hell of a book. I can't wait for the finish. It will be an all-nighter—I will stay up late not wanting to lay it down.

—Snuff Garrett
Music Publisher and Former A&R Director for
Liberty Records, 1959-1966

Country music historians owe a debt of gratitude to Lawton Jiles for this long overdue inside look at how the Bakersfield Sound came to be and who contributed to it. Lawton knew or worked with most of the singers and musicians who put the city and its sound on the map and he brings their stories to life in this thoroughly fascinating and entertaining book. It's a bit!

—Steve Hunt
Senior Editor of Pasadena Star-News

The Birth of the Bakersfield Sound

A HONKY TONK ATTITUDE

LAWTON JILES

YorkshirePublishing
www.yorkshirepublishing.com
Write Now.

ISBN: 978-1-948282-5-12
The Birth of the Bakersfield Sound
Copyright © 2013 by Lawton Jiles

Yorkshire Publishing
3207 South Norwood Avenue
Tulsa, Oklahoma 74135
www.YorkshirePublishing.com
918.394.2665

ACKNOWLEDGEMENTS

This project was a labor of love, both for music and for the people involved in the birth of the Bakersfield Sound. Through several years of writing, this book was completed with the help of a number of people, many of them friends with whom I had the pleasure of sharing the stage.

First, I wish to thank my loving wife, Ruth, for her continued urging to finish this project. We are blessed to have a full and busy life and a large family. Finding the time to write was not always easy, but she made every effort to help make this book possible.

A very special thank you to my granddaughter, Elizabeth Turner, to whom I owe so much. Elizabeth was a great help with my research for this project as she tracked down names, numbers and bios of some of the artists. And, she's a great boss.

Thank you to my son, Michael, for his technical contribution and support, and to his wife, Rebecca, for her assistance with editing and feedback. Thank you to my son, Casey, for his help and suggestions in researching this project.

Thank you to my sons, Jerry and Kenny, and our daughters, Marguerite and Melinda, for their encouragement, and to my many grandchildren for their inspiration.

I offer my thanks to God for the life He has given me, that I might enjoy so many wonderful experiences.

There were a number of personal interviews conducted to make this book a reality. I spent several hours with my old friend Bill Woods; Cliffie Stone, who was going to write the foreword, but passed away before we finished; Henry Sharpe; Red Simpson; Marlene Rich Dunivent, the wife of Don Rich; Oscar Whittington; Cliff Crofford; Rose Maddox; and Doyle Holly. I also had the pleasure of conversing with folks like Jeff Nickell, former director of the Kern County Museum and a fine country and gospel writer himself.

Thank you to Jennifer Barbour for her help typing the information from the interview tapes. Thanks are also due to Rachel Thomas for her help with typing.

A special thanks to the folks who head up the Bakersfield Country Music Museum for their offer of help in stories, pictures, etc. President Jerry Bowen, Fred McCaa, Inez Savage, Tommy Hays, and Rockwell, who owns Trouts and the Blackboard stages, thank you all for your support.

A big thank you to Snuff Garrett for his insight and comments on the career of Cliff Crofford, in which he played such a big part.

Various books and magazines proved valuable resources, including: *In the Country of Country* by Nicholas Dawidoff, *Working Man Blues* by Gerald W. Haslam, and *San Antonio Rose* and *The Life of Bob Wills*, both by Charles B. Townsend. The book, *Memories: The*

Autobiography of Ralph Emery by Tom Carter was also informative. Interviews with Fred and Rose Maddox were helpful and enjoyable.

Other reference sources were Merle Haggard's *Sing Me Back Home*, written with Peggy Russell; *The Bakersfield Californian* by Robert Price; *Country Song Round Up*; *Music City News*; *Ramblin' Rose*, by Jonny Whiteside. Rose gave me the book during one interview saying, "Here this is the story of my life!" Country Music Association; Academy of Country Music; and The Bakersfield Library.

When folks caught wind of what I was doing, I received many calls and letters with stories and articles, and I appreciate those people's contributions. This book was written to honor a very special time in country music, and to recall those people with whom I worked, shared the stage, and built memories.

A special thank you goes to Steve Hunt, the sports editor of the San Gabriel Press, for his great job editing my mistakes. He is a songwriter and the husband of Luann Hunt, a recording artist and a great writer and newspaper reporter. Luann has recorded some of my songs, and I am grateful for that and the success we have both enjoyed.

I also wish to thank Steve for being very helpful with this project from the start. We took a trip to Bakersfield and spent a day searching for information at the Bakersfield Library, where folks there were so helpful to us.

I apologize for the failure to mention many deserving folks who played a part in this page of history.

It is with a heavy heart that I think of or hear names that deserve to be mentioned, names of disc jockeys, booking agents, club owners, sponsors, etc., but time and the inability to recall many of the names and events during these years have played a part. I have tried to tell the story the best I can and write down the research and interview information I have gathered over the years.

I wish to thank everyone once again for their kind support.

CONTENTS

FOREWORD

One day, back long ago when Lawton's hair was brown and curly, he said to his wife, Ruth, "I'm gonna write a book on Bakersfield Music, so you'll have to work a little harder to cover some of my schedule." After a long struggle to get that book written, he is coming down to the bottom line, so he asked me to write the foreword. I hope it meets his approval.

Lawton has worked long and hard with a lot of research and personal interviews to tell the story of the many entertainers and musicians that have been a part of the Bakersfield music scene. Buster Simpson; the drummer Johnny Cuviello; Bill Woods, who heads up the band at the Blackboard Café; Johnny Barnett, who played the Lucky Spot for twelve or more years; Fuzzy and Bonnie Owens; the unforgettable Lewis Tally, who mortgaged his home to save Tally Records; and many, many others are a part of this book.

I moved to Bakersfield in June of 1949, and got my first job with Bill Woods' band. We had a gig in McFarland, California at the 99 Café, and we also did a short radio show on week days on KAFY. It was an early morning program, so we would sit up all night, often sleeping in the car after working the club in McFarland. Over the years, I worked clubs, radio, dances, television, and recording sessions with almost all of the artists mentioned in this book. Many of them have recorded my songs, and I have been so honored.

I have been asked many times over the years to explain the Bakersfield Sound. Although I worked in the pop field and survived the rock era, my interest was always in country music. I was never able to define the Bakersfield Sound. Lawton has explained its beginning and the folks that helped bring it to its peak of popularity better than any explanation I have seen. We have talked often about this special time in country music, and I was excited when I read the transcript and learned how he put it all together.

Lawton grew up in Delano, California and knows firsthand about the Bakersfield Sound, having been a part of it himself for many years. Lawton and I are life members of the Bakersfield Country Music Museum. Lawton has also been a very close and personal friend of mine for many years. My wife Maxine and I wish to thank and congratulate Lawton on this fine work.

—Cliff Crofford

INTRODUCTION

Buck Owens passed away in his sleep on March 25, 2006 at his ranch home outside of Bakersfield. The funeral services were held at the Valley Baptist Church in Bakersfield, one of the largest churches in the city, and the church was filled to capacity, with some folks standing in the rear. The pews were filled with friends, entertainers, and admirers of Buck, people he had helped along the way and many whose careers had been inspired and influenced by his work.

When I heard the news of his death, many thoughts and feelings ran through my mind. Buck and I had been friends since 1952, and my thoughts were drawn back to those early years and the struggles he and all musicians had to go through. I thought of the time I spent with him as his bandleader and how we had to work to get a crowd. I recalled how much time and effort he put into getting his record played in the beginning and how it all paid off as he went on to become one of the biggest stars in country music.

Buck's success would never have been possible without the inspiration, help, and support of the many talented and dedicated people in his life. Producer Ken Nelson, in-your-face steel guitarist Ralph Mooney, and fiddler Don Rich played vital roles in Buck's early career as they recorded and performed together to build names for themselves. His wife, Phyllis, was a hard-working, no-nonsense lady with a conservative approach to business who gave her complete support to Buck and the band members. She would talk about her husband's homesick, late-night phone calls when his work took him far from home. The separation from his family brought on by those long trips was often more difficult for him than the financial burden.

After Buck's death, I thought a lot about these times and of the heights he would reach later in his career. He had a lot of help and support from a great number of people, but his energy and drive always made everyone around him work just a little harder. He expected total loyalty and would not hesitate to remove anyone who did not support his way of doing things. Buck was the spark that would light the fire that became the Bakersfield Sound, a hard-driving mix of country, rockabilly, honky-tonk, and western swing styles.

Buck Owens went from the humble beginnings of often having to fight for crowds and airtime, to the monumental success of owning several radio, TV stations and the Crystal Palace in Bakersfield, which includes a museum of many of his treasures. Buck was a performer who wanted to please his public, and he was a man who had no idea he was changing country music forever. He never played to impress other musicians; he played for the crowd. He said it best himself, "I'd like just to be remembered as a guy that came along and did his music, did his best and showed up on time, clean and ready to do the job, wrote a few songs, and had a hell of a time." Those of us in the band in those early years would never have imagined that we were watching country music being reinvented.

The spotlight was on Buck Owens and he did not fail or falter. His all-out effort brought forth the work that would be known as the Bakersfield Sound. Many folks have given support and contributions to the Sound, but it was Buck who gave it the breath of life.

THE BIRTHPLACE

In the early 1800s, long before the truck stops and honky tonks, cotton fields and oil rigs, Bakersfield, California was a largely uninhabitable swampland due to the runoff from the Tehachapi Mountains that covered the land for much of the year. The runoff would split at what is now known as Panorama Heights, giving Bakersfield the appearance of an island. The San Joaquin Valley is now one of the country's richest agricultural and oil regions, with a history rich in musical heritage as well.

In the pioneer period of California, a man of vision named Colonel Thomas Baker was the original owner and founder of what is now called Bakersfield. Colonel Baker was born in 1810 in Muskingum County, Ohio, and grew up on a farm where he became familiar with agriculture and gained a practical knowledge of surveying. He also studied the law and wanted to become a lawyer, but he later moved to what would soon become Iowa territory, where he became the first U.S. District attorney in the territory. In 1841, he was nominated as a colonel for the Iowa Territory Militia. He was elected to the legislature there and served as president of the senate, thus becoming ex-officio the first Lieutenant Governor of Iowa. Many of the important laws still on the statute book of Iowa were devised and drafted by Thomas Baker.

While he was prominent and successful in Iowa, political turmoil and his love for adventure eventually inspired him to travel westward. In the fall of 1850, he arrived in Benicia, California, and after a short stay, he traveled on to Stockton. In 1852, he moved to Tulare County, where he helped lay out the town of Visalia. It was there that he met and married Miss Ellen Whalen in 1857.

In 1855, he was elected to represent his district in the state legislature. He served well in that capacity, and in 1858, he was appointed Receiver for the United States Land Office under the administration of President James Buchanan. During the legislative sessions of 1861 and 1862, he served as a senator from Fresno and Tulare counties.

During this time, in partnership with Harvey Brown, Baker acquired the Swamp Land Franchise granted to the Montgomery Brothers, and began his reclaiming efforts in 1862. Along with Edward Tibbet and a contract from the state of California, he immediately began a plan to control the Kern River and its flow through Bakersfield. With the river harnessed, Colonel Baker knew the land would be perfect for a major city. He also foresaw Bakersfield's oil production capabilities and the likelihood that rail travel would link the city to both Northern and Southern California.

Baker proved to be a man of incredible vision. The Kern River oil boom began in 1899, and to this day, oil continues to be one of Bakersfield's biggest industries.

In the 1870's, when the Southern Pacific Railroad began laying tracks through the middle of the state to connect Southern California with Northern California, the rails crossed through the Tehachapi mountains at the exact spot Baker predicted.

The railroad brought major changes to Bakersfield. Eager for passengers' fees, the railroad worked dutifully with all of California's real estate brokers. Ads were run throughout the East and Midwest advertising the great opportunities and health benefits awaiting in the West, ideas appealing to adventurous Americans and newly arrived American immigrants. Bakersfield grew quickly, along with the entire south end of San Joaquin Valley. By 1871, the newly formed community of more than 600 residents began referring to their lots as located in the east end, south end, central section, etc. of "Baker's Field." The town that was once known as "the island" had become "Baker's Field," soon to be simply "Bakersfield."

Baker was a man of broad vision who offered a kind-hearted, helpful, unwearied hospitality to strangers, even when hard-pressed. He would give newcomers a sack of flour when he didn't have means to buy another one for his family. Many times he would give away his lots to promising but poor young businessmen. He donated some of the best business locations because he knew the town would need good, honest businessmen in order to prosper. He entertained travelers in his adobe house, fed their horses in his corral, and never charged them room and board. Both the new railroad and Baker's generosity fostered the rapid population growth of the community, and it was that generosity that set the tone for Bakersfield's musical heritage.

Baker's son, Thomas A. Baker, wrote that the family moved into a log home on what is now Nineteenth Street. He recalled that after a few days there, a captain of a wagon train moving through the Sierras came by the house with a crate containing six hens and a rooster. He said, "Mrs. Baker, I know you would like a start in chickens." The clucking and cock-a-doodle-do-ing of those animals was probably some of the first singing heard in Bakersfield.

As time went on, music from piano recitals and fiddle-fueled square dances filled the air around Baker's house. Colonel Baker's house became the first honky tonk.

Colonel Thomas Baker passed away at the age of 62 on November 24, 1872. This was a memorable date in history, as it was the same day of death as Horace Greely, famous for his words, "Go West, young man."

The population of Bakersfield grew rapidly in the twentieth century due to the large amount of movement in and through California by migrant workers affected by the Dust Bowl, and people coming to work in the many California shipyards. Because of its location between San Francisco and Los Angeles, Bakersfield became a connection between Northern and Southern California.

The entertainment in Bakersfield grew and developed with the population. The migrant workers brought music with them from the Midwest, Arkansas, Oklahoma, Texas, Kansas, and Missouri. By the twenties and thirties, many theatre troupes and bands were appearing in Bakersfield on their way to Sacramento and San Francisco. At this time, Bob Wills was creating country versions of big band swing songs, and featuring vocalists with new styles that caught on quickly. By 1940, there were dance halls and various clubs wanting entertainment. Everyone wanted to dance, so big bands were the craze, and bands like The Dorsey's, Benny Goodman, Paul Whiteman, Glenn Miller, and many small bands traveled to California.

Bakersfield became a place to search for a dream of prosperity in the San Joaquin Valley, and a gathering place for music. It was the perfect spot for a new sound to be born, a place where people from many different states would meet and share stories of poverty, heartbreak, dreams, and offer songs handed down from their forefathers. All of this fostered the need for a hard-driving music with a honky-tonk sound that would kindle the spirits of these folks in their new land.

THE BEGINNING

Americans have constantly had adventurous spirits, always dreaming of a better, happier way of life, traveling the world looking for their own rainbow. Music has fueled the American dream in a special way because a song is more than just meaningful words on paper. The melody speaks to each person on a deeper level, giving the song significance beyond the lyrics. Music styles will change with almost every record as the needs of the fans change and as each recording artist develops a unique sound.

The need for an upbeat, hard-driving sound was strong in California in the 1930s. The migration from the Midwest to the West Coast during the Great Depression brought a great many people who were looking for work and a new way of life. These folks wanted music that would cheer them up and remind them of the home and family they had left behind. This migration grew in the late thirties as World War II was starting and the nation was beginning to arm for war. Thousands of people flocked to the West Coast to build ships for the battles to come.

At the time, big bands that performed pop music across the land were winners, selling millions of records and introducing a style that had become uniquely

American music. Small bands were also popular, playing swing music and a western style based on radio and movies featuring Gene Autry, Roy Rogers, and others.

A huge influence in country music at that time was Jimmy Rogers. Even in his short life, Jimmy's writing, performing, and recording styles all affected the industry tremendously. His influence brought a lot of new talent to the music world, and even today, many country artists pay tribute to Jimmy Rogers.

Bob Wills made millions of friends in the thirties by playing dances with live radio shows in Texas and Oklahoma. His popularity grew exceptionally fast as he recorded and toured with Tommy Duncan and his Texas Playboys. Their popularity carried over to California as well, prompting Wills to take up residence in Sacramento for a while in the mid-forties at the famous Wills Point. Wills had a swing style that seemed to fit the needs of the San Joaquin valley folks. It's not difficult to imagine a young migrant or soldier from Oklahoma listening to "Take Me Back to Tulsa" for the first time.

First Lieutenant Hugh C. Minter was a World War I veteran who died in an airplane crash at March Field in July of 1932. Bakersfield honored his sacrifice by dedicating Minter Field army air corps base to his memory. Many of Minter's relatives are still in the area, and one of his relatives, Toby Minter, was a drummer with the Valley Rhythm Boys for three years.

On February 7, 1942, operations began at Minter Field, located alongside the railroad and Highway 99. As the number of cadets increased, Minter Field became one of the largest pilot training bases on the West Coast, and utilized such practice fields as Delano, Lost Hills, Pond Famosa, Wasco, and a strip that once existed in Dunlap. More than 11,000 air cadets who graduated from Minter Field later went to war. As a kid, I remember watching them all fill the sky as they practiced their pilot skills. It was a daily show with a lot of noise.

During their stay, the soldiers were looking for entertainment. This was a great thing for Bakersfield, and the nightclub scene and local dance halls sprang up during this time. Big bands could tour and soldiers could find entertainment and meet local girls. Many would return after the war and settle in the valley.

The last half of the forties brought a big change in music. Big bands were fading out, demand was rising for ballad singers, and individual artists were becoming very popular. Such performers could travel faster with fewer instruments and less personnel than the big bands, so the door of opportunity was open for singers in the pop field like Crosby, Nat King Cole, Margaret Whiting and other solo acts.

When World War II ended, country music developed. We now had Ernest Tubb, T. Texas Tyler, and a number of others doing hard honky-tonk style songs with great success. There were great ballad singers as well, such as Eddy Arnold, Burl Ives, and Hank Williams.

The war's end brought new challenges for soldiers coming home, who found themselves in need of jobs, housing, furniture, appliances, cars, and entertainment for themselves and their families. They were in a hurry to make up for the years away from home. The war was over, and people needed songs to remind them of lost love, of home and family and friends left behind in service, of their hometown in another state, and songs to remind them of America and how good it was to be home.

It was truly a new frontier, a real opportunity for those up to the challenge, and a great arena for country singers nationwide to hone their craft. A performer could draw a crowd in any bar around, and learn how to perform and read a crowd to give them what they wanted to hear. Many folks traveled the land and played for tips, food, drink, and room and board. Radio offered them support and airtime to give them a chance to use their talent and salesmanship to develop an audience. Recording companies were also ready to jump in, having learned a lesson from Ralph Peer in the thirties, a man who traveled the country and discovered such special talents as Jimmy Rogers, the Carter family and others.

And so the stage was set in the late forties for radio to sound out a string of new artists like Hank Williams, Ernest Tubb, Maddox Brothers and Rose, Eddy Arnold, Roy Acuff, George Morgan, Hank Thompson, Bob Wills, Pee Wee King, Little Jimmy Dickens, and Red Foley. Crowds wanted to dance to these songs, dream over a cold drink, and either relive old memories or make new ones. Many returning soldiers were still unmarried, and this was a tremendous way to meet people. The parents of many of today's baby boomers came together in such settings, and still have memories of a song that forever they will call "our song," a sentiment worth more than gold to any songwriter.

This was the beginning of a music that would fill a need for many people. It was music to dance to, and music to ease loneliness. It was music that could inspire, or music to idly hum while toiling on the farms and oil fields of the mighty San Joaquin. It was music with a honky-tonk attitude.

THE ARCHITECT—
BOB WILLS

Bob Wills was born in Kosse, Texas in 1905. At age ten, Bob joined his father, champion fiddler "Uncle John" Wills, to play barn dances, parties and special fiddle events. He lived in migrant labor camps, picked cotton, and worked as a farmer and barber, but Bob was a bit of a reckless young man. After being arrested for public rowdiness, he left home and joined a medicine show where he learned how to entertain and hold a crowd with music styles like blues, Dixieland, and swing.

In 1929 while visiting Fort Worth, Texas, Bob met a guitar player by the name of Herman Arnspiger and a singer named Milton Brown. Milton had a band called Milton Brown and His Musical Brownies, and some say it was the first Western swing band. Two years later, the three began advertising flour on a radio program on a Fort Worth station sponsored by W. Lee O'Daniel. They were known as The Light Crust Doughboys.

Bob grew restless during this time, and drank uncontrollably. In 1933, he was fired from the Doughboys after missing a broadcast, so he moved to Waco to start his own band. He took with him a young singer in the band by the name of Tommy Duncan. In time, Bob would come to refer to Tommy often as his "right hand man."

Their new band was called the Texas Playboys. Bob had learned much about running a band, about radio and entertaining a crowd, but life was not easy. Each time the Texas Playboys found a new station, W. Lee O' Daniel, their former employer and a very powerful man in Texas, would get them fired.

Frustrated with their radio problems, Wills, Duncan and the other members of the band moved to Tulsa, Oklahoma. They took a job on KVOO, a 50,000-watt station in Tulsa, no doubt the greatest move in the lifetime of Bob Wills, the Texas Playboys, and Western swing. From 1934 to 1941, they performed daily on KVOO. In 1935, Wills hired Smokey Dacus, who became the first drummer in a major country band. With a vast audience, KVOO was the perfect avenue to expand Wills' popularity. In addition to the radio exposure, Bob and the Texas Playboys also played to huge crowds nightly at Cains Academy Ballroom in Tulsa.

Bob worked on dance arrangements, fusing Dixieland Jazz with big band sounds, adding horns, fiddles, hot guitar licks, and the steel guitar. He incorporated these styles with polkas, blues, waltzes, and swing. His music, mixed with Duncan's vocals, appealed to many cultures. Wills' famous "Ah-hah, San Antone!" caught on in the early forties, along with the band's honky- tonk attitude. After 10 years of leading the Texas Playboys, Wills boasted, "We're the most versatile band in the country." And he was right.

My father was a big fan of Bob Wills and took me to see him in Sallisaw, Oklahoma, in 1940. The band played behind the Carl Frix General Store, advertising flour. Although I was just a kid, I was blown away by the band with their white Stetson hats and their big amplified sound, Tommy Duncan's singing, Bob's yelling, and all the "Haw!" I was amazed at Leon McAuliffe on the steel guitar. I had never seen or heard of a steel guitar, and though my mother played a dobro, the steel was something else. On the way home, I told my dad, "That's what I want to do."

The Dust Bowl of the thirties had caused a westward migration of people looking for a better life. The war years that followed brought job opportunities in defense work, and agriculture brought more jobs and more migration. The end of the war found many soldiers settling in New Mexico, Arizona, California, and Oregon. In 1947, they found Bob Wills and the Texas Playboys there, too. He had moved to Sacramento, California, purchased the Aragon Ballroom, and called it Wills Point. The San Joaquin Valley was ready!

Bob and the Texas Playboys toured the Southwest and did a daily radio show over KFBK, a 50,000-watt station in Sacramento, California. They did other shows on radio by transcription, some 15- and 30-minute broadcasts over Fresno and Bakersfield stations at midday. In the late forties, my father and I would pick up these broadcasts.

Will's best and most famous recordings were between the late thirties and the early fifties, and influenced most every musician that came out of Bakersfield. He appeared in the city many times, mostly at Oildale's famous Beardsley Ballroom. I went to see the band there in the early fifties. In 1960, my brother Johnny saw them at Pumpkin Center on Taft Highway, and the band did "Let the Teardrops Fall" that night, a song written by Buster Beam and myself that was recorded by Patsy Cline.

In 1948, there was some disagreement between Bob Wills and Tommy Duncan about dates Bob had missed, and Bob fired Tommy. After sixteen years working together, Bob's right-hand man was gone. Bob left California shortly after and returned to Oklahoma, leaving Wills Point in the care of Tiny Moore and his band in the hands of his brother, Billy Jack. Many of the band members settled in California, from Fresno to Sacramento.

Bob's influence remained strong in California music, even during the emergence of such stars as Merle Haggard. In the 1970s, Haggard cut a Bob Wills tribute album that featured many of the original Texas Playboys. Bill Woods told me about going to Texas that December, 1973 on what I suppose was his last recording session. Merle Haggard was there, and did some of the vocals. During this time, Wills fell ill and passed away in 1975.

It is hard to identify just how important Bob Wills was to the eventual birth of the Bakersfield Sound. There was a strong desire to dance to live music, and Bob was there to provide it. He laid the groundwork for the necessary talents to be developed, and he lived to see the Bakersfield Sound come into its own. He must have heard his influence, and I'm sure he was proud of the boys from Bakersfield.

THE RIGHT HAND MAN—
TOMMY DUNCAN

Thomas "Tommy" Duncan was born to Jack and Edna Duncan on January 11, 1911 in Whitney, Texas, a small town south of Dallas. He was the eighth of fourteen children. As a teenager, Tommy left Whitney to live with his cousins, some of whom were country musicians. Tommy ran with them and developing an interest in the music business there in West Texas.

In the early thirties, young singers were influenced by Bing Crosby's wide range of music and Jimmy Rogers' ramblin' blues and honky-tonk style. Tommy was also influenced by the yodeling of Emmett Miller.

His break came in 1932 when guitarist Herman Arnspiger heard Tommy sing and play the guitar at a root beer stand. Arnspiger mentioned Tommy to Bob Wills, who was then with the Light Crust Doughboys band. Tommy auditioned for Wills and joined the Doughboys on September 21, 1932. He was twenty-one years old when he became Bob Wills' "right hand man."

The Doughboys had a tough schedule, and keeping up took its toll. Personal appearances, radio broadcasts, and dance schedules made a normal life impossible, and relationships and marriages suffered.

When the Doughboys eventually disbanded, Bob and Tommy ended up in Tulsa, Oklahoma where Tommy became the front man for Bob Wills' new band, The Texas Playboys. As part of the Playboys, Tommy's entertaining style developed. He would excite the crowd by stomping on the piano keys, "perhaps to cover up his poor playing," Bill Woods later joked.

Tommy became a star, and the Playboys' record sales began to climb. People loved Bob's antics on the records, and everyone wanted to hear Tommy Duncan sing. Tommy became an idol to many young musicians searching for the right "attitude" in their music. Bob and Tommy could do it all, be it swing, blues, jazz, big band, or honky-tonk. Many of the young musicians they influenced, talents such as Johnny Gimble, Julian McCullough, Noel Boggs, and Johnny Cuviello, also known as the "Texas Drummer Boy," would never forget Tommy Duncan's influence during their careers in music. He inspired musicians and fans alike. His sound had a honky tonk attitude that would later be called "the Bakersfield Sound."

Tommy worked with Bob Wills and the Texas Playboys from 1932 to 1948. They traveled the country, appeared in several movies, and did many radio shows, both live and by transcription. During some of these shows, Bob would be on a drinking binge, leaving Tommy and the boys to cover for him and put up with promoters' complaints. They were paid a fixed scale instead of receiving a percentage. When Tommy expressed his unhappiness with all of this in 1948, Bob Wills fired him after sixteen years together.

Tommy started his second career by securing a new manager and a recording contract with Capitol Records. He formed a new band that featured some of the former Texas Playboys members and named the new group the Western Allstars. The band was made up of some of the best in Western Swing: Noel Boggs on steel guitar, Joe Holley playing a left-handed fiddle, Tommy's little brother Glynn Duncan on bass, guitarist Jimmy Wyble, and Millard Kelso on piano.

In the fall of 1948, Millard Kelso decided to leave the Allstars. Tommy had met Bakersfield local Bill Woods on prior occasions, and Tommy gave him an audition at the Beardsley Ballroom. This event changed country music in Bakersfield in a profound way because one of its own was involved. I was still in high school in Delano, California when I went to see The Tommy Duncan Show in November of '49. Bill Woods was probably 20 years old then, playing piano and a fiddle tune.

Bill was a local hero who would become known throughout the country. In Dallas, on the way to a Fort Worth show, the Allstars stopped at a red light and a pedestrian walked up to the window and asked, "Do you have ol' Bill Woods in there?" Tommy pulled off his hat, slapped his knee, and said, "If I ever go someplace where they don't know Bill Woods I will eat this hat."

Tommy's only hit record was on his second session with Capitol Records. It was Jimmy Rogers' "Gamblin' Polka Dot Blues," and it reached number eight on the Billboard charts.

The Allstars traveled extensively through the Midwest, Southwest, and West in a specially built army stretch-out bus, a vehicle somewhere between a bus and a limousine. Bill Woods said it looked like two Chevrolets welded together. For a while, they had good crowds. The hit record, however, was not enough to keep them going.

Big band business was falling off. Antennas were showing up everywhere now, and TV was looming larger and larger as entertainment dollars were saved to buy TV sets. Crowds were dwindling because people were spending more time in clubs. Honky tonk singers were doing well, and more clubs were opening up throughout the West.

Capitol dropped Tommy in 1950, and he dissolved the Allstars and hit the road, performing with local bands. In 1951, he signed with Intro Records where he made some good records, but had no hits. He also recorded with Coral Records in 1954 with some results, but nothing that showed up on the charts.

Tommy loved Bakersfield and the San Joaquin Valley. He and Bill Woods were special friends, and helped each other in many ways. Bill gained credibility in the industry because he worked for Tommy in 1948, and now Bill was booking acts at the Blackboard and other venues in and around Bakersfield, giving Tommy access to the area.

Tommy was popular with the fans and the musicians who had grown up with his music. He was their hero and it was always a special time when he was in town. Many would have him in their homes for a meal after a show.

On several occasions, Bill Woods would take me to the place Tommy was staying for a visit. There was always a guitar present and someone would pick it up to sound out a new idea. Tommy always had a comment. I recall one time someone was singing out of his range. Tommy said, "Change the key. That's why there are different keys," and everyone had a big laugh. Tommy knew how to make and please friends. It was entertaining to hear him speak and tell stories about the great musicians he had worked with on the road.

Tommy continued working as a solo act through most of the fifties. Bob Wills, who had not spoken to Tommy Duncan since he fired Tommy in 1948, called Tommy in 1959. Bob had not been able to find a singer to replace Tommy, and his fans had lost interest. Tommy agreed to sing for Wills, and they drew large crowds again. They signed with Liberty Records in 1960, where they recorded "Heart to Heart Talk," a top-10 song. In 1961, they had another moderate hit, "The Image of Me." Soon, though, Bob reverted to his old ways of not showing up for shows. Tommy couldn't take it anymore and left to start up his solo career again. Though he had little in the way of success after that point, Tommy Duncan was still loved and respected as a hero to many musicians.

He and his wife, Marie, moved to Mariposa, California, to a 260- acre cattle ranch. Tommy worked hard on the road and on the ranch, and for a man in his fifties, this was too much. He went on medication for heart disease, and fell to a fatal heart attack on July 24, 1967.

Tommy, along with Bob Wills and the Texas Playboys, was a major catalyst in the creation of the Bakersfield Sound. It saddens me that neither Bob nor Tommy lived to enjoy the gain in popularity of Western Swing in the late seventies, but they both saw the sound come into its own and surely took pride in their part in its birth. They had laid the groundwork for many bands to come and opened the door on the honky-tonk attitude.

THE FATHER OF THE SOUND AND THE SOUND'S BEST FRIEND—BILL WOODS

Bill Woods was born in Denison, Texas, nine miles from Buck Owens' birthplace in Sherman, Texas. Though they did not know each other at that time, their paths were destined to cross. With the help of his mother, who was able to teach him three chords, Bill Woods taught himself to play the guitar. His father was a minister, and his mother was the church pianist. She also played the accordion, which she taught to Bill's oldest sister as well. When Bill was twelve and his sister was ten, their family performed on a radio show that his father had in Denison.

The Woods family later moved to Longview and lived in what was called a tent camp. There was an oil boom at the time, and it was difficult for families to find housing. "If you had a tent with a wooden floor, you were really livin'," Bill says. Next door to them lived a Mexican family that would gather out front every evening to play music. "I just loved that kind of music," Bill says, and so he asked them if he could sit in. "I learned a lot right there," he recalls, and it would influence him the rest of his career.

While Bill was in high school, he and his family moved to Arvin, California, a town near Bakersfield. Bill was too young to play in clubs, but he formed a little four-piece band and played for assemblies. They played old Western-type music, Columbus Stockade Blues and the like, and they recorded for the first time on a wire recorder. The first song they recorded was Bob Wills' new "San Antonio Rose." It was for nothing more than their own personal use, of course, but it was a beginning.

Bill's family soon moved to Visalia, California where his uncle worked as a carpenter. Bill worked with him on the construction of a facility to train fighter pilots at Dinuba Air Force Base. He also had a part-time job mixing mud for a cement block company in Visalia.

When he left there, Bill went to Los Angeles, where Spade Cooley and Dude Martin were kings. He tried to find a job with an airplane factory so he could hang around the scene, but not only was he too young to play music, Bill was too young to work in the factories. So, he returned to Visalia to finish his junior year of high school.

A year later, Bill left Visalia for Richmond, California, and started working in the shipyards. He spent some time there in a band called the Arizona Wranglers, headed by Elwyn Cross out of Fresno. The band was made up of a fiddle player named Dave Stogner, a female singer named Levina Lee, and Bill on the upright bass.

Bill became a lead man in the shipyards, working as a boiler maker with a crew of 32. Even though he was still a teenager, he became very good at handling a crew, and the management skills he developed in the shipyards would benefit him later in his music career.

While Bill was working in the shipyards, the country was caught up in war bond efforts and using entertainment to gather a crowd. Twice a week, government personnel would come out and take anyone who played music to different shipyards during lunch hour to play shows and sell war bonds. Bill used these opportunities to gain further experience.

After his time with the Arizona Wranglers and managing his crew at the shipyard, Bill was ready to start his own band. He took a job at a place called Maple Hall. His band manager was Joe Dobson, and according to Bill, Joe had worked with Jimmy Werk, the writer of "Making Believe."

Bill moved around for the next few years, playing here and there. He met Herb Henson at the Fresno Barn in Fresno, California. Later the two would rejoin to reach unbelievable goals. He also went back to Bakersfield and became good friends with Oscar Whittington, who was learning to play the fiddle. The two of them would go down to a club called Rhythm Rancho on Saturday nights and sit in with such musicians as Odel Johnson, his son Sonny, Johnny Ash, and the guitarist Jimmy Jeffries. Bill remembers Jimmy Jeffries as quite the character, with his face painted up every night with something that looked like lipstick.

Right after World War II, Bill left the Rhythm Rancho and went to the Saddle Club in Las Vegas. He played there a year or so with his friend Tex

Marshall, then returned to Bakersfield, and went to the Clover Club.

At the Clover Club, Bill started the Orange Blossom Playboys. He had Jack Trent on piano, Buster Simpson, Red Simpson's brother, on bass, and Lloyd Green from the Ford Lewis Band on guitar and fiddle. Bill recalls, "Lloyd played 'The Orange Blossom Special' better than anyone I ever heard on the fiddle," inspiring the band's moniker. Bill also hired Billy Mize at the Clover Club.

One night at the Clover Club, Jimmy Thomason, a fiddler who had been working with Governor Jimmy Davis of Louisiana, walked up to the bandstand. As was always the case, Bill invited him up to do a couple of numbers. Jimmy would later recall he had visited several other clubs and "[Bill was] the only one that would talk to me and let me set in. They acted like they were afraid I would get their job." Bill met and nurtured many friends in the music business with his open demeanor.

When Jimmy Davis was out of office, he moved to Palm Springs and opened a club there. He wanted Thomason to join him, and since Jimmy was also looking for a piano player, Thomason recommended Bill Woods. Davis hired Bill, and off Bill and Jimmy went to Palm Springs. Bill played piano and doubled on mandolin, and Thomason played fiddle. Bill says Davis had a beautiful place in Palm Springs with a bar "the size of my yard."

The band would play for square dancing during the weeknights, and on weekends they would have special shows with covered wagons. They would bring people out from Hollywood, make a campfire, and cook a big breakfast for all the stars. Bill says it was "quite a deal." They had Las Vegas style parades, and Bill says, "We played the El Dorado parades there too." Bill and Jimmy Thomason stayed almost a year.

Davis went back to Louisiana, and Bill Woods and Jimmy Thomason returned to Bakersfield where they did DJ work on local radio stations. Woods was still a young man in his early twenties, but he had gathered much experience in marketing and as a musician.

Around this time, Woods began performing at the 99 Café in McFarland with band members Dude Wheeler on guitar and Kurt Webb on Bass. Cliff Crofford joined later on trumpet. They would work until one o'clock in the morning, drive to Bakersfield, wait in their car, and appear on KAFY Radio at 5:00 a.m.

Not long after, they had a chance to record Cliff on Marble Records with Bill on piano and Billy Mize on steel. Tommy Duncan came to town around that time, and Bill Woods played that record for him. Hearing Woods playing piano and Billy Mize playing steel stirred interest in Tommy, who had recently left Bob Wills and now had his own band. When Tommy's piano player, Millard Kelso, had to leave the band for family reasons, Tommy called Woods and Mize for auditions. Woods auditioned with Millard Kelso standing at his side, and Woods said, "I don't know how I got the job, I was so nervous." Tommy sent Woods a telegram a week later, asking him to meet him in Santa Paula, California and join the band. Billy Mize also joined the band later.

They toured the West and Midwest with Tommy's band. On one tour, Bill recalled that they were going to play at an army base in Salinas, and Tommy wanted to visit a friend who owned a place there called the Buckaroo Bar. So, Bill Woods and Ernie Ball, nineteen years old at the time, went along. They walked in, sat down, and heard the most beautiful voice coming from another room. Bill asked Tommy's friend if it was a jukebox he was hearing, and the friend replied no, it was "some damn wino." Bill went into the next room and there was a young Ferlin Husky, who was going by "Terry Preston" at that time. Bill recalls, "I started talking to him. He told me his sad story, in a crying drunk kind of way. His girlfriend had run off with a trapeze artist that had come through town, and he was crying in his beer."

Bill said, "'Me, Ernie Ball, Glen, Duncan, and Billy Mize are all here, about two blocks up the street at the hotel. I would like you to meet them.' So we started walking up the street. We passed one of those photo booths. He had on a nice leather jacket. He said, 'How about me selling you this leather jacket for five dollars?'

I said, 'Man, it's winter, you need your jacket. I'll give you five dollars.' So we took the pictures." Bill still has those pictures.

They went on to the hotel, not knowing yet that Terry Preston was a comedian. He started doing tricks, still half-drunk, picking up chairs with his teeth and doing other crazy things. After he left, the band members started making fun of him. But Bill said, "Let me tell you right now: one of these days that ol' boy's gonna be big, one of the biggest names in the business." Woods would connect with Ferlin sometime later.

After about a year with Tommy Duncan, and not long after Mize left the band, Woods decided to head a new direction. Herb Henson had called Bill and asked him to come back to Bakersfield to take over the band at the Blackboard Café. Bill talked to the owner, Frank Zabaleta, and a deal was struck. Bill returned to Bakersfield, took over the band, and began doing DJ work at KBIS with a live radio show on Sunday afternoon starting at three o'clock from the Blackboard.

It was at that time that Bill crossed paths with Ferlin Husky again. With Bill's aid, Ferlin took up a DJ position at KBIS and started an amateur show at Rainbow Gardens on Friday and Saturday nights. The show was a big hit.

During this time, 21-year-old Leonard Sipes came to check out all that was going on in Bakersfield. Bill and Ferlin sized him up and saw potential. Ferlin talked Leonard into staying in Bakersfield, where he helped Leonard develop his singing style and begin a serious writing career.

This was the start of a community of creativity that would build into something phenomenal. Ferlin, who still went by Terry Preston at the time, was an idea man, and, just like Bill Woods, he was looking for promotional ideas. Herb Henson, another sales-minded person, also helped with the promotion of the Sound at this time. All the while, they still recorded and worked the Blackboard and other local events together.

Bill Woods, Fuzzy Owen, Lewis Talley, and Billy Mize were playing at different clubs, but all were bound together by friendship and an eagerness to learn. There was a building a couple of doors down from the Blackboard that had a little beverage counter in the basement. After work, all of these musicians would meet there until dawn, working on ideas, telling jokes, and having fun with each other. They had a little one-track recorder there. Hillbilly Barton had written a song called "Dear John Letter," first recorded by Woods and Rita Goodwin. Bonnie Owens and Fuzzy Owen recorded it on 78 rpm, with Woods playing the fiddle for both recordings. The song, although only on small labels, earned a lot of airplay and local interest.

Bill Woods, Lewis Talley, Fuzzy Owen, and Ferlin Husky went to Capitol Records to show the song to Ken Nelson, and, after much debate, it was decided that Capitol would record the song. Jean Shepard would sing, and Ferlin Husky would do the narration. The song became a number one hit and helped put Bakersfield on the map. The Bakersfield Sound was on the move, and Bill Woods had played a huge role in bringing the pieces together.

In 1953, country music came to television with Jimmy Thomason's show on KBAK-TV and Cousin Herb Henson's "The Trading Post Show" on KERO. Cousin Herb's team was made up of Herb on piano, Billy Mize on steel, Johnny Cuviello on drums, young Carlton Ellis on vocals, and Bill Woods on guitar and vocals. It later took on other performers, some from local clubs, like Fuzzy Owen, Lewis Talley, Bonnie Owens, Roy Nichols, and Dallas Frazier, with many guest stars making appearances to promote their shows at some of the local clubs. "The Trading Post Show" and its performers became extremely popular during its 10-year run.

Bill Woods and his fellow musicians were like rock stars. I recall one time in 1954, Woods was helping me do some demo work at Ed Smizer's studio. I met Bill at his house on Saturday morning, and we had a cup of coffee then headed to the studio in his new Cadillac. We drove a few blocks before we realized that two cars were following us, each with at least four girls in them, and they followed us all the way to the studio. I wanted to urge them to go home, but even though he did not know them, Bill invited them inside to watch us record. Ed Smizer gave his reluctant okay for them to stay, so the girls sat down on the floor along the walls, and we went to work. We were there for at least two hours, and those girls stayed the entire time. That's how popular those musicians were, due in no small part to the sort of open friendliness Bill offered that day.

Bill Woods continued to work at the Blackboard. He did much of the booking for the club and had guest stars every Wednesday and Thursday night, some of which would go on to become country legends, like Tex Ritter, Ernie Ford, Johnny Cash, Merle Travis, Johnny Bond, Gene Autry, Ernest Tubb and Lefty Frizzell. Even Barbara Mandrell, Patsy Cline, Johnny Horton, George Jones, Bob Wills, Tommy Duncan, Rose and

Cal Maddox, Webb Pierce, Little Jimmy Dickens, the Everly Brothers, and many others worked the club.

Bill helped and advised anyone who would ask. In 1951, Bill hired Buck Owens for the Blackboard, and in the early sixties Bill had a young Merle Haggard work the Blackboard on his night off. Bill recalled that it took a lot of encouragement to convince both Buck and Merle to sing because all they wanted to do was play their guitars.

Bill also had a hand in shaping the talent of 19-year-old guitar player Phil Baugh. Phil was a truck driver who had heard some of the things that were going on in Bakersfield. He stopped by the Blackboard one day and met Bill Woods. When Phil told him he played guitar, Bill invited him to set in. Phil really put on a show. At one point, Bill put his guitar down and told the band to step down from the bandstand and let Phil be the show. On Sunday, Bill repeated the routine when Phil came back down for the radio show, and a star was made.

Phil played Bakersfield for a while with Bill's help. Eventually, Phil went to Los Angeles for a couple of years, then on to a successful tenure in Nashville as a session player and performer for the rest of his life. For a while, he was the featured guitar player for Ralph Emery on "Pop Goes the Country."

Woods started a record label with Hillbilly Barton and Chris Christensen called Bakersfield Records, and he invited me to record a couple of my songs. Bill produced and played stand-up bass, Buck Owens played lead guitar, Johnny Cuviello played drums, and

I played rhythm guitar. Once, Buck asked me how old I was. I said, "I'll be twenty-five in December," which was only a month away at the time. Buck had turned twenty-six in October. I remember him telling Bill, "Everyone I see is younger than me."

Bill said to him, "Just keep working at it. You have plenty of time to make it in the business." I knew then that I was not the only one depending on Bill's counsel.

When performers would become discouraged and begin to look for greener pastures, Bill would always talk with them and encourage them. Bill was their best friend, always there to lend an ear, always offering his opinion when asked. He never put himself first or insisted on his name being on any contract. If someone succeeded, he was as happy as they were, and Woods touched many careers and many lives. He hired and worked with nearly all of the musicians who contributed to the birth of the Bakersfield Sound, helping them find jobs, housing, transportation, instruments, clothes, or whatever they needed.

From the beginning, his bands always had a raw, hard driving sound with honky-tonk attitude. His band made it through the transitional period of the mid-fifties of early rock and roll and the rhythm and blues period. Bill hired Don Markham on trumpet and saxophone, Buck Owens on guitar, Henry Sharp on drums, and Lawrence Williams on piano. Their music kept the crowds coming back all through this period until more country sounds came around in the late fifties with Ray Price recordings. George Jones and others brought back the fiddles and steel guitars, thus opening the doors for Buck Owens.

In the early seventies, Merle Haggard recorded a song called "Bill Woods from Bakersfield," written by Red Simpson. Sometime later, Simpson recorded his own version of the song. Bill was very proud of Merle. He played the piano on the Merle Haggard Show for a while, and he was with Merle in the '70s when they went to Texas for the Bob Wills tribute.

Bill had injured his back some years earlier in an accident driving a car for a friend in a destruction derby, another of his long-time hobbies, and the back injury affected his hands. He retired with his wife Angela, and at the time of our last interview they had five children and seven grandchildren between them, one child named Merle Haggard Woods, and a daughter named Tommie named after Tommy Duncan.

On three different occasions, Bill and I sat in his backyard at a big picnic table doing interviews on tape, talking of the old days and old friends. It was a marvelous time. Though he has never received the credit he deserved for helping so many people throughout his life, Bill will never be forgotten by those who knew him.

Bill Woods passed away on April 30, 2000 after a long illness. My wife and I attended his service at The Valley Baptist Church in Bakersfield where the pews were filled with friends, fans, family, and many of the musicians he had known and helped. Bill's many influences in the birth of the Bakersfield Sound can still be heard on country radio today, and the music world will long remember him.

HE CAME FROM ALABAMA WITH A DAUGHTER ON HIS KNEE—MADDOX BROTHERS AND ROSE

Charlie Maddox was a fine banjo player, so it wouldn't come as any surprise if he came to California with his seven-year-old daughter and a banjo on his knee.

The Maddox family were all born in or near Boaz, Alabama, located in the Sand Mountain region of the state where the Louvin Brothers and the Delmore Brothers were also born. Charlie Maddox married Lulu Gertrude Smith in 1910. They became sharecrop farmers in a poor part of the country, living in a wooden shack outside of Boaz on a few acres of land. There they bore seven children: Clifford; Alta; John Calvin, or "Cal;" Fred R.; Kenneth C., known as "Don" or "Don Juan;" Roselea Arbana, the "Rose of Alabama;" and Henry Ford, named after the auto maker and later called "Friendly Henry" or "the working girl's friend."

Their journey to California in the throes of the Great Depression is a story of struggle and dogged determination. Lulu was a short, stout woman with an independent spirit and an natural take-charge leadership attitude. She was determined to leave Alabama and come West to what the advertisements dubbed "the land of milk and honey." So Charlie, Lulu, and the five youngest of their seven children set out, hitchhiking and hopping aboard westbound freight trains. Traveling like this was not unheard of in those times, and because this family had young children with them, people would offer help when they could.

It took them three weeks of travel through all manner of weather to get from Boaz, Alabama to Glendale, California, a remarkable 2,000-mile journey. They were half-starved and sleep-deprived, but they had survived by stopping to rest in hobo camps, and sometimes Charlie and his son Cal would go out and work day jobs to help their plight. Charlie was offered a job at a restaurant in Glendale, but Lulu refused, insisting they were headed for the gold fields up in Sonora.

So onward they went via freight car to Bakersfield. April of 1933 was the first time the Maddox brothers and Rose set foot on Bakersfield soil. In that moment, not one of them, not even Lulu in her wildest dreams could have imagined what the future would hold for their family in the world of hillbilly music. She expected them to accomplish much in life, but the level of fame and fortune they would attain a few short years later would make Lulu a modern day prophet.

The family found that Bakersfield, like Alabama, was hit hard by the Depression. They spent one week in Bakersfield, living off of meals from the Salvation Army, then they headed up to the gold country. They arrived in Oakland at the end of April and found a sight they had not yet seen anywhere on their journey. Pipe City, it was called, where hobos lived in huge concrete pipes. There was even a city council, complete with a city hall that was headquartered in three tents. One of the head hobos gave them his pipe.

The seven Maddoxes moved into the pipe, putting blankets on the front for privacy. The Oakland Tribune came down and did a story on the family—"Family Roams U.S. Looking for Work" the headline read, complete with their family picture.

My wife, Ruth, Kathy Robertson, and I had dinner with Rose in Irwindale, California in early 1988. We talked about some of these times and how their mother Lulu looked out for them. She enjoyed telling stories about her mom. She went on and on about her mom paying cash for Cadillacs for the band.

Lulu did not like all that close scrutiny. Some people would offer donations, but she wanted to succeed on her own. The family hopped another freight headed into the hills of the Sierra Nevadas, known as the "mother lode" country, where they moved into a vacant cabin there. After a couple weeks of panning upstream, they found less than a dollar's worth of gold dust. They were stuck 2,500 miles from the hills of Boaz, Alabama, in the hills of the Sierra Nevadas, but their plight remained the same. Lulu was at her wit's end, and her dreams were dimmed.

The family eventually took one more freight ride to Modesto where Charlie got a job on the Talbot Ranch. They reasoned that if they were able to buy a

1931 Model A Ford, they would be able to move up and down the state, following whatever fruit or cotton there was to pick.

The oldest son, Cliff, was still in Alabama with his wife Gordie, and times were getting harder there. Cliff and Gordie did like the rest of the family and stuck out their thumbs and headed west. At that time, Cliff was the only musician in the family besides Charlie. He had learned his music from Charlie's brother, Foncy Maddox, a well-known traveling musician and music teacher in the Southeast. Cliff would often work with him, learning from Foncy and gaining experience. Cliff would not part with his guitar, and carried it with him on the trip west.

In California, Cliff met up with a cousin, Kurt Tony, and together they began playing and singing. Before long, they were broadcasting on KTRB Radio in Modesto. All during this time, Cal was playing around on the guitar with Cliff's help and Rose was singing any song she could. She would often enter singing contests at school, and Cliff and Cal would accompany her with guitars. This was the beginning of something big.

The family, now doing better and working steady, bought a radio they could tune in to XERA or XERB in Mexico. They would listen to the Carter Family, Patsy Montana, and people like the Sons of the Pioneers, whose harmonies enchanted Rose. One Sunday, Rose saw the Sons of the Pioneers at the Strand Theatre in Modesto, and she was star struck. She said that event made up her mind. After seeing The Pioneers and a young Roy

Rogers, hearing the yodeling and the harmonies, she knew what she wanted to do with her life.

By the fall of 1937, the family was doing pretty well, able to pay rent, but still working the crops. Fred had gone to a rodeo and was caught up with the performance of a band there, Logan Laam and the Hoppy Hay Seeds. Rumor had it they were paid $100. Fred considered all of this, discussed it with the family, and it was decided that they should go into the music business.

Fast-talking Fred got them guest spots on KGDM Radio in Stockton. Armed with his natural charm and talent as a salesman, Fred went to Rice's Furniture Store in Modesto in search of a sponsor. He drawled on for a half an hour with his pitch before Mr. Rice said, "Okay, I'll put you on the air, but I want you to do the talking. Just hearing you talk is worth a million dollars." Mr. Rice got Fred, Cliff, and Rose on Modesto's KTRB five mornings per week, from 6:30 to 7:00 a.m. It is reported that in their first week they received 1,000 fan letters. Rose was eleven years old.

The Maddox family started going to towns that featured rodeos, playing for tips in beer bars. They performed like this all up and down the San Joaquin Valley, always getting back to Modesto by 6:30 a.m. to do the radio show, sometimes traveling 300 miles or more. All the while, they were creating their own hillbilly sound that was a combination of folk and traditional country with a honky-tonk attitude. It was up in Susanville, not long after they started on KTRB, that they heard Woody and Jack Guthrie, two cousins, on a broadcast over Los Angeles radio station KFVD. The Maddoxes found the songs fit them very well, and "The Philadelphia Lawyer" and "If You Ain't Got the Do-Re-Me" became forever tied to the Maddox Brothers and Rose.

Mama pooled all of the family money, Papa's included, and put it into a band fund used to maintain the Model A Ford and to buy stage clothes for the group. Rose, now twelve, would wear a cowgirl outfit, a fringed skirt with a belt, scarf, hat, and boots, and the boys dressed in hats, boots, satin cowboy shirts, bandana ties and new jeans, and wore long sideburns. Mama was the boss, and she kept the group sharp, ready, and motivated.

They were making their mark on the San Joaquin Valley, from Bakersfield all the way to Sacramento. Fred was developing a radio personality while he promoted engagements over the radio, and with his natural gift for talking, exaggerated drawl, and entertaining personality, he was being imitated more and more. The family was now broadcasting over two stations, KTRB Modesto and KGDM in Stockton, doing an average of 15 shows weekly. Around that time, they began looking for ways to reach a larger audience.

In 1939, they headed for a hillbilly band competition at the Sacramento State Fair, an event Rose spoke of a couple years before her death. When I asked if they were nervous, she answered, "No. We didn't even think of being nervous; we just expected to win. We just loaded everything in the Model A and headed for the state fair." They sang "Sally, Let Your Bangs Hang

Down." With the combination of rocking rhythm and teasing lyrics, along with all the clowning the group was doing, the crowd was caught up in the Maddox magic. None of the other fifteen groups stood a chance.

The prize was a one-year contract on radio station KFBK in Sacramento, part of the McClatchy Broadcast Network that all but ruled the San Joaquin Valley and stretched to every corner of California, including Hollywood. This gave the Maddoxes steady work, an opportunity to develop as entertainers, and most of all, the exposure they had hoped for. They were still broadcasting over KGDM in Stockton, so the San Joaquin Valley was tuned in and turned on to the Maddox Brothers and Rose.

They seemed to know what the fans wanted. The family knew themselves, and found songs that suited them. When the show would start, fans would stand as close as they could get to the bandstand, often covering half of the dance floor. During this time, most of the shows were performed with Fred on bass, Cal on guitar and harmonica, Rose on vocals, and sometimes Don would play fiddle. Cliff had moved to Modesto, and he would join them if the band made an appearance close by.

In 1940, things were going great for the Maddox Brothers and Rose. They had gone from cotton pickers to radio stars, from near starvation to fame, and life was good. They were in constant demand by 1941, traveling up and down the state like busy bees. The start of World War II in December of 1941 would change things for the Maddox family.

After December seventh, when the Japanese bombed Pearl Harbor, the Maddox boys all registered for the draft. Fred and Cal were called into the army in 1942. Fred became a mess sergeant in the Pacific, where he organized a band, named them the Khaki Mountaineers, and was able to tug along a bass fiddle on his Pacific theatre travels. It was here that he developed his slap style of bass playing. Cal went to Australia.

Don went into the service in 1943 and was stationed in India. Cliff was exempt because of Rheumatic fever, and henry was too young for the draft. Without Fred's voice and energy, things were not the same, and the radio show ended.

Through the war years, Rose kept trying to work, but there seemed to be little demand for a still very young girl singer. She did some work with Dave Stogner at the Big Fresno Barn. Lulu, anxious to do business again, was encouraging Henry to play mandolin. He worked hard on the instrument, and progressed well. The brothers sent nearly all of their money home, and Lulu put it away to be used in starting the band again.

Fred was discharged in November 1945. Cal got home before Christmas of that year, and Don returned in February of 1946. Christmastime was a time of celebration, and a time for making plans for the band.

With Cal playing his guitar and harmonica on a yoke, Henry on lead, and Rose on vocals, they did their first broadcast on KGDM in Stockton, California on December 29, 1945. Their sound had changed in several ways. They were older, for one, and Henry's mandolin gave them a different driving sound. They were now delivering a postwar honky-tonk attitude, and their theme was "I Want to Live and Love." They would turn the music down, and Fred would step up to the microphone and do his best imitation of himself: "Yes sir, and howdy folks, how are y'all? This afternoon give us a great big smile, will ya?"

We lived in Delano, California at that time, and each morning my dad would have their program on. I would listen to some of their foolishness before going to school. I was interested in songs like, "The Philadelphia Lawyer," "Live and Love Again," and "Gathering Flowers." My dad would sing these songs, and I learned them as I began to play the guitar.

In the late forties, now in high school, I went to see them as often as I could, never thinking I would get to know them. The way they dressed, and the way they acted out each song was something to see and hear. Boy, were they loud! In the mid-forties, they took on two hired hands, Jimmy Winkle, known as "Jimmy with the Light Brown Hair," on lead guitar, and Bud "Honky-Tonkin'" Duncan on steel guitar. In 1949, I went to see the show in Tulare. By then, they also had a young guitar player named Roy Nichols who would, over the next couple years, take their music to new heights. Roy became very closely tied to the Bakersfield Sound, and added to its birth.

The mid- to late- forties were the peak of popularity for the Maddox Brothers and Rose. Their music was of greater quality, and they were providing the type of entertainment that was needed at the end of World War II with all of the soldiers returning. Migration was greater than ever, and clubs were springing up everywhere to accommodate the entertainment needs of a growing population. The Bakersfield clubs supported and utilized radio, and in turn, radio stations supported Bakersfield music fully. Many of the clubs' bandleaders would have 15-minute DJ shows, so a mix of fan radio and club owner support helped make the birth of the Bakersfield Sound possible.

On many occasions during the later forties and fifties, The Maddox Brothers and Rose worked the Blackboard Café, a small café where truckers would stop for coffee or breakfast. Folks could read the blackboard for messages, events that were going on, or search for job openings. In 1951, the café was remodeled and made much larger, complete with the addition of a grand wooden dance floor. Over the next few years, it would become known as the "cradle" of the Bakersfield Sound. The Maddox Brothers and Rose were well received there and at other Bakersfield locations, such as Pumpkin Center Barn Dance and the Rainbow Gardens.

The Maddox Brothers and Rose's contribution was vital to the birth of the Bakersfield Sound because of their ability to entertain in a variety of ways, be it comedy, honky-tonk songs, or rocking rhythms. They had turned the San Joaquin Valley upside down and created the desire to go out and find live music. Memories of this family and this band are still held dear to the country folks who had the opportunity to hear and see them perform.

MR. PERSONALITY—
BILLY MIZE

Billy Mize was born William Robert Mize in Kansas City, Kansas on April 29, 1929. When he was still a young boy, his family moved to Rubidoux, California, a city near Riverside where he attended both grammar school and high school. His father accepted a steel guitar in a trade at his used furniture business and gave it to Billy on his 18th birthday. He fell in love with the instrument and worked hard to learn how to play. His singing came quite naturally, and Billy found inspiration in Tommy Duncan's vocal style and music.

By the time Billy arrived in Bakersfield, he was ready to go. He began performing at the Sad Sack, and it was not long before Bill Woods got word that a new man was in town who sounded like Tommy Duncan. Bill, who was working at the Clover Club at the time, said, "Tell him when he gets a break to come see me." Shortly after they met, the two joined forces.

Billy later got a radio spot on KAFY doing a 15-minute show as "Billy the Kid." The show was on the air for three years.

I first heard Billy Mize in 1950, the same year he spent a few months in The Western All Stars, his hero Tommy Duncan's band. Afterward, he returned to Bakersfield and worked at local clubs before joining the band at the Lucky Spot. There he worked for many years alongside Cliff Crofford, Johnny Barnett, and a host of other sidemen.

Buck Owens came to Bakersfield looking for work in 1951, but he had hocked his guitar for living expenses. Jimmy Thompson hired him for a weekend gig, and Buck said, "I borrowed a guitar from Billy Mize," and Oscar Whittington said he loaned Buck a white shirt and a western string tie for the job.

In 1953, television came to Bakersfield. Jimmy Thompson began his show in September on KBAK TV Channel 29. A few days later, Cousin Herb with Billy Mize and Bill Woods began "The Trading Post Show" on KERO TV Channel 10. Cousin Herb played the piano and was the emcee, Bill Woods was on guitar, fiddle, and sometimes piano; Billy Mize played steel guitar and did vocals; and Johnny Cuviello was on drums. A teenage Carlton Ellis joined the show, and a little later, Dallas Frazier joined as well. The show was a huge success, and the cast became so popular that they could draw a crowd anywhere they went.

In the beginning, Cousin Herb, Bill Woods, and Billy Mize were partners, but Cousin Herb eventually took over as manager, and Bill Woods and Billy Mize pulled out under the agreement that they would become paid band members. They worked the show about a year before Billy and Cliff Crofford began their own show on KBAK TV called "The Chuck Wagon Gang."

A year later, they met a young Merle Haggard and gave him his first television experience.

By 1957, Billy's records had spread to radio stations in Los Angeles and throughout the Midwest. Billy and Cliff were invited to Compton, California to join "The Town Hall Party," a big television show full of stars on Saturday nights. This opportunity provided quite a bit of exposure.

That same year, Billy and Cliff began work on "The Cal Worthington Show," hosted by Sammi Masters.

On November 26, 1963, Billy's longtime friend and one-time business partner, Herb Henson, had a fatal heart attack at the age of 38. Herb had been hosting "The Trading Post Show" on KERO TV for a full decade. When he passed away, Billy was called to take over the daily duties from 5:00 p.m. until 5:45 p.m.

Billy's travel increased greatly as he drove to dates from Bakersfield to the Los Angeles area. As if this were not enough, in 1963 he began hosting Gene Autry's "Melody Ranch Show" on Saturdays.

Billy played a role in the founding of the Academy of Country Music. In 1965, he won Country Music's Best Television Personality Award. The next year, he took the same award again, and also won Most Promising Male Vocalist. That same year, he started "The Billy Mize Show" in Bakersfield.

All of his time spent driving was helping Billy write songs. In 1966, Dean Martin recorded three of Billy's songs, all in the same day. In 1967, he won the Best Television Personality award for the third time, and in

1968, his band, The Tennesseans, won the Academy of Country Music's Band of the Year award.

Billy volunteered and spent a great deal of time in fundraiser programs for handicapped children. In the mid-seventies, he was made an honorary member of the Kern County Sheriff's mounted posse. He also filmed television pilot shows, one with Merle Haggard, and another with Marty Robbins.

In 1983, Billy recorded and released "Billy Mize Salute to Swing," a tribute to Tommy Duncan featuring the original Texas Playboys. The Tennesseans went on to win the Band of the Year award again from the Academy of Country Music another two years running. In 1988, he was inducted into the Western Swing Society Hall of Fame.

In 1991, Billy suffered a stroke that affected his speech. Though he speaks slowly, Billy still plays the guitar and sits in with local bands from time to time.

March 20, 1994 was proclaimed Billy Mize Day with celebrations all around Bakersfield. Musicians began to gather early at The Casa Royale, a nightclub south of Bakersfield on Union Avenue. The ballroom filled quickly with fans and entertainers wanting to see Billy again. Billy stayed in front of the bandstand wearing in his Stetson hat, his Western clothes, and his ever-winning smile.

The entertainers there were some of Bakersfield's finest. Tommy Hays served as Master of Ceremonies. Jimmy Sanders played with his band, the Stage Riders, and his father, the great Jelly Sanders, joined in for some tunes. Bill Woods, the man who could be called the Godfather of Bakersfield, and Billy's one-time boss, partner, and a long-time friend was there shaking hands with the crowd. Tommy Duncan's brother, Glen Duncan performed, and Oscar Whittington and his son Richard were there, too. Bonnie Owens joined in with some familiar tunes that pleased the crowd.

At the celebrations, Billy's brother Buddy read a telegram from Merle Haggard, who was across the country on tour, but wanted to send along his congratulations to Billy. Later in the afternoon, someone mentioned that Buck Owens was there. Buck brought along the Buckaroos, and the party was soon on. Their first song was "Act Naturally." Buck did several of his hit songs, but he refused to steal the spotlight from Billy Mize on his special day.

They performed a song written by Billy called "Who'll Buy the Wine." Billy walked up to the bandstand, hoping to speak, but the crowd could not hear his words. Buck quieted the crowd, and Billy spoke to thank Buck for coming out. Buck finished his program with "The Streets of Bakersfield." What a day of recognition it was for Billy Mize.

On April 28th, 2009, another party was held at the Crystal Palace on Billy's 80th birthday that drew many of Bakersfield music's elite to celebrate. Billy was there, looking handsome as ever. Many of his old friends who had been at the party in 1994 at Casa Royal had passed away by then, but my wife Ruth and I, Cliff Crofford and his wife Maxine, Red Simpson and his wife Joyce, and a number of other Bakersfield musicians attended.

Bobby and Sandee Durham and the Durham Band performed with special guests. The Legard Twins performed first, then Billy's longtime friend Merle Haggard and the Strangers took the Crystal Palace stage, and the party was on. Merle's young son Benny was featured on lead guitar and really put on a guitar clinic. It was a great evening and a huge tribute to Billy.

Billy was a big influence to all of the musicians because he was so professional in his dress and his stage presence. He, along with Cliff Crofford, influenced a lot of singers in voice control, and he led the way in honky-tonk songs in the style of Tommy Duncan. He could croon with the best and knew how to use the microphone for effect. He knew how to please a dance crowd and hold them, and he was a high personality for years with many fans.

THE QUIET MAN—
CLIFF CROFFORD

Clifton Thomas Crofford was born on December 12, 1929 in Rochester, Texas to Clifton and Faye Crofford. Cliff's father passed away from a ruptured appendix at the age of twenty-one, three months before Cliff's birth. Faye was just nineteen at the time. Cliff was raised by his mother and his grandfather, Thomas.

When Cliff was nine years old, his mother met a young man named Levi Davis. She thought Levi would make a good stepfather, and the two were married in 1938. Cliff's sister, Rebecca Sue, was born in 1941. In early 1942, the family moved to San Diego where his stepfather worked in an aircraft factory during the early war years. Cliff's youngest sister, Patricia Lynn, was born in 1943.

Cliff developed a strong interest in music early on in his life. He won a singing contest back in Rochester, Texas when he was just four years old, taking home a bag of groceries as his prize. At age eleven, he was listening to and being influenced by all of the big band sounds on the radio at the time. He would watch Spade Cooley, Tex Williams, Bob Wills, and others perform at the Mission Beach Ballroom, unaware that he would one day become friends with those men.

Cliff entered a six-week singing contest in Linda Vista. On the final show, Cliff sang "Don't Sweetheart Me" and was chosen as the winner. His prize was to appear on a radio station at the US Grant Hotel.

When Cliff was twelve, his mother took him to a pawnshop to look at the guitars, but it was instead a trumpet that sparked his interest. He ended up paying $50 and going home with a used trumpet with a hole in it. His junior high school had no band class, so Cliff had to learn the trumpet on his own by ear. He was in his first year of high school in La Jolla, California before he had his first band lessons and learned how to read some music. A few weeks after his first lessons, he was promoted to second chair ahead of seven or eight other trumpet players, some of them second- and third-year students.

In 1945, Cliff's stepfather joined the Army Tank Corp., and Cliff's mom decided to return to Texas to be near her family. When Cliff returned to Rochester, Texas halfway through his freshman year, the school had no band program, so he continued with his self-taught method. In his junior year, Rochester hired a music teacher, and he began to learn how to read music again. Four or five of the boys in the band, including Cliff, were also on the football team. When halftime came around, they would leave the team to do their part with the band, then come back and finish playing the game.

After completing high school, Cliff returned to California and enrolled in junior college in Riverside. After finishing the school year in June 1949, Cliff decided to take a vacation to Reno, Nevada. Cliff's friend, a steel player named Tex Worell, suggested that Cliff give Bill Woods a call on his trip through Bakersfield. Worell had worked with Bill Woods in the Jimmy Davis Band in Palm Springs. Cliff had not heard of Bill Woods, but Worell said Bill knew what was going on and might know of a playing job for the summer that Cliff could do before returning to college.

Cliff did call Bill Woods on his way through Bakersfield, and Bill invited him out to his house in Oildale, California. As Woods recalls, "The skinny 19-year-old kid knocked on my door, introduced himself, said he played trumpet, and was working with Tex Worell." Bill invited Cliff to sit in with him at the 99 Café in McFarland. They were playing with three pieces at the time, and Bill said he would see if they would go for four. Cliff played a good trumpet and was a very good singer, landing him a job at the 99 Café.

On a night off, Woods took Cliff over to the Clover Club, a popular nightclub at the time. Woods introduced him to piano player Cousin Herb Henson, steel player Billy Mize, guitarist Johnny McIntee, and Eddy Clark, a stand up bass player. Cliff also became acquainted with Buster Simpson, Tex Marshal and Jack Trent at another club called the Lucky Spot, Fuzzy Owen and his cousin Lewis Talley at the Blackboard Café, and Woods' best friend Oscar Whittington.

This group would come to be the cornerstone of the Bakersfield Sound.

There was still a lot of Western music in Bakersfield, but this group was young, highly motivated, and serious about their music. They brought a new energy to the music in Bakersfield with their hard driving honky-tonk sound influenced by T. Texas Tyler, Earnest Tubb, Hank Williams, Hank Thompson, Tommy Duncan, and the easy listening music of Eddy Arnold that pleased the dance crowds.

Cliff bought a small trailer house from Billy Mize's mother in the same park Bill Woods lived in. He never did make it to the vacation in Reno that summer, and he didn't return to college in the fall of 1949. His heart had been captured by the Bakersfield music scene.

Cliff, though still young, was fulfilling a dream of playing music. He and Billy Mize were learning to write at this time, with the constant encouragement of Bill Woods. Bill would use the poor man's publishing routine of sealing the lyrics in an envelope and mailing it back to themselves. They recorded two of Cliff's songs and two of Mize's songs on a wire recorder.

Cliff played in several bands at the Lucky Spot and the Blackboard Café. He worked with young players like Gene Moles, Johnny Barnett, Gene McGraudy, and Johnny Cuviello, the one time drummer for Bob Wills and the original Texas Drummer Boy. Cliff devoted his full time to performing, writing, and recording on local labels. One of those early labels was Modern Records.

In 1951, Cliff met the love of his life, Maxine, and they were married in Las Vegas. At twenty-one years of age, Cliff found himself with a whole new set of responsibilities, as he became an instant father to Maxine's young son. His love for his new bride and her total support for him gave Cliff the strength he needed.

Cliff was one of the first people to appear on television in the early 1950s when Bakersfield was entering the television era. He worked on a mid-day music variety show emceed by George Day that featured himself, Jean Shepherd, and others.

In September 1953, Jimmy Thomason sold his idea for a television show to KBAK Channel 29. The station was not sure that country music would find an audience. The band was made up of Jimmy on fiddle, his wife Louise on vocals, Cliff on trumpet and vocals, Ray Heath on drums, and Gene Moles on guitar. A week later, Cousin Herb Henson's show began on KERO Channel 10. Cliff began recording with Fuzzy Owen and Lewis Talley on the Tally Label, working weekends with Cousin Herb, and often appearing with Cousin Ebb at the Pumpkin Center.

"The Louise and Jimmy Thomason Show" ended when Jimmy returned to Waco, Texas, so in 1956, Cliff and Billy Mize began their own show on Channel 29. The band was made up of Buck Owens on guitar, Jack Trent on piano, Ray Heath on drums, Mize on vocals and steel guitar, and Cliff on vocals and trumpet. In 1957, with some of Cliff's records now on the radio and Mize's recordings on Decca Records also doing well on the radio, the two men were invited to join "The Town Hall Party" in Compton, California. They were still playing at the Lucky Spot, but traveled each weekend to the Los Angeles area for the show.

The Everly Brothers were a big act during this period, so Cliff and Billy teamed up and did a duo act that became very popular in the Southland. They did this for two years before accepting a job at the Foothill Club in Long Beach, California, owned by Charlie and Bonnie Price. With Cliff on vocals and bass and Billy on vocals and steel guitar, they worked with Gordon Terry on guitar and fiddle and Mike Fury on drums. At this point, Cliff and Billy moved their families to the Los Angeles area. Cliff worked the club six nights a week and did "The Town Hall Party" TV show on Saturdays for a while before taking a leave to join Roy Nichols on a Johnny Cash tour.

After the Johnny Cash tour, Cliff returned to the Foothill Club where a new guitar player named Tommy Allsup was performing. Tommy was a well-traveled musician with many hours of recording experience under his belt and a lot of friends in the music business, including Cliffie Stone and Snuff Garrett. Tommy introduced Cliff to both men and explained Cliff's writing skills. Snuff was the A&R Director for Liberty Records from 1958 to 1966 and had worked with Buddy Holly and many rock and roll artists and was the first to hire Phil Spector, who would later become a huge producer in pop music.

As he was hanging around the Liberty office one day in the early sixties, Snuff told Cliff he needed a song titled "Chip Chip" for a session they were doing with Gene McDaniels. Cliff accepted the challenge and worked most of the night writing the song. The next day he and Tommy Allsup made a demo of "Chip Chip." McDaniels recorded the song, Snuff produced it, and the song went to Number 1 on the pop charts.

Meanwhile, Cliff had been working on a song called "Old Rivers." Early on, he had given the song to Cliffie Stone before he began his work with Liberty, having written the song with Johnny Cash in mind. Stone had never recorded it. Snuff told Cliff that if he could get the song back, Snuff would record it, so Cliff got the song back and Snuff went to work. When Snuff believed in something, he would not relent. He knew songs and was great at picking a hit song. This song, however, presented a challenge because it was a project with only narration and no singing. As Snuff would explain later, one producer was saying "I need an artist who can sing his butt off," but Snuff was saying, "I need an artist who can talk his butt off!"

This was all during the time of the John Glenn flight into space in the early sixties and someone had written a song titled "The Epic Ride of John Glenn." The idea was timely and had to be done while the iron was hot. Al Bennett was pushing Snuff to get it recorded quickly, but Snuff was not sold on the song and could not find anyone for the project.

Snuff continued to work hard on finding someone to do the narration for "Old Rivers." He approached the actor Tony Curtis, who said he had to go to New York for three weeks and would do it when he got back. A few days later Snuff was talking to a friend about his frustrations in finding someone for "The Epic

Ride of John Glenn" and the pressure he was getting from management. That friend called Walter Brennan, Walter called Snuff, and the rest, as they say, is history.

Snuff produced the record and he put Cliff in the booth with Walter to direct the narration. Walter would refer to Cliff as Mr. DeMille, a reference to the famous movie director. Snuff said the sessions were all three-hour timed sessions. He used two hours and fifty minutes on "Old Rivers" and ten minutes on "The Epic Ride of John Glenn."

Management at Liberty was not sold on "Old Rivers," but Snuff certainly was. He took the song to a disc jockey, Chuck Blore, on KHJ Los Angeles. Blore liked it, saying if Snuff released it, he would make it his top pick of the week. The project became a huge hit world over. Snuff left his mark on the last line, "Old Rivers and me" by having Walter redo the line and put a tear in "me." Anyone who hears this record can almost feel the tear fall. Cliff was now in demand as a successful songwriter.

As "Chip Chip" was making its way down in the charts, "Old Rivers" was climbing up, on its way to becoming a Number 1 smash. Cliff was working some with The Crickets at this time, and doing recording sessions with Glen Campbell, Bobby Vee, and Jerry Ivan. Buddy Knox recorded Cliff's "Dear Abbey," and Johnny Burnett recorded Cliff's "That's the Reason You See Me the Way I Am."

There was a new edge on contemporary music with the arrival of the Beatles to the U.S. in the sixties, creating a few lean years for country music. During this time, Cliff and Billy did some recording for Dore Records and some recording for Challenge. They also recorded two sides on Liberty Records produced by Tommy Allsup, "Louisiana Sand" and "Don't Look Now," an old Earnest Tubb song.

Cliff returned to some club dates and special appearances while he enjoyed some successes with his songs, such as Gary Lewis' "Let Me Tell Your Fortune" and "The Best Man," Gene McDaniels' "Chip Chip," and Vicky Lawrence's "The Other Man."

Cliff made several trips to Nashville to make recordings for a possible contract on Columbia. On one occasion, he was to meet Chet Atkins for an interview in the RCA building, but reluctance set in as he was walking up to Chet's office. Chet was a virtuoso, and Cliff could not bring himself to play in front of him. He walked up to the door, which was closed, but he did not knock. He walked up and down a couple of times, then returned to the studio. He later saw Chet walk over, grab his overcoat, and go home.

Back in California, Cliff continued to work the Foothill Club in Long Beach and write songs for whomever he could. In the late sixties, Snuffy was producing a Cher project and he picked one of Cliff's songs, "Melody." It was the "B" side to "Half Breed." The record was a million-seller.

In the seventies, Cliff was still working clubs and special shows and writing many songs for movies. In 1979, Snuff Garrett called and wanted some songs for a movie he was doing with Clint Eastwood called "Every Which Way but Loose." Cliff wrote "Send Me Down to Tucson," a Number 1 hit song recorded by Mel Tillis, and "I Can't Say No to a Truck Drivin' Man," recorded by Carol Chase. He also wrote and sang "Monkey See Monkey Do" for the soundtrack and appeared in the movie.

The next movie was a Burt Reynolds project, "Smokey and the Bandit II." Roy Rogers did "Concrete Cowboy" and the Statler Brothers did "Charlotte's Webb," a Number 1 song.

Then came Clint Eastwood's "Any Which Way You Can." Cliff was a co-writer on a Fats Domino number called "Whiskey Heaven" and wrote "Orangutan Hall of Fame." Cliff recorded and performed the song on the soundtrack and appeared in the movie.

Cliff continued to write for movies, co-writing "Beauty's Theme" performed by Farrah Fossett in Burt Reynolds' "Cannon Ball Run II." Cliff also had songs in Eastwood's "Bronco Billy." He co-wrote "Bar Room Buddies," a Number 1 song performed by Clint Eastwood and Merle Haggard, "Star Dust Cowboy" by the Reinsmen Quartet, and "Bayou Lullaby" by Penny Dehaven.

The next movie he worked with Eastwood on was "Honky Tonk Man." He wrote "One Fiddle Two Fiddles," performed by Ray Price with Johnny Gimbel and Gordon Terry on fiddles, and "When the Blues Come Around this Evening," performed by Linda Hopkins with Cliff playing trumpet on the soundtrack.

Cliff and Garrett were hot in the early eighties. Cliff had a couple of cuts by Ray Price, "Willie Write Me a Song" and "Living Her Life in a Song." Shortly after "Honky Tonk Man," Garrett suffered a stroke and had to cut back on his efforts. Cliff still performed some, and continued his writing.

In the mid-eighties, Cliff began to slow down. He built a vacation home in Wawona, California, in Yosemite Park and began to spend more time with his family.

Cliff has won many awards and enjoyed many Top 10 songs. Among his highest ranked songs are "Old Rivers," "Chip Chip," "Send Me Down to Tucson," "Bar Room Buddies," and "Charlotte's Web," all of which won both a BMI award and were ranked Number 1 on the Billboard charts. Cliff also wrote "Texas State of Mind," which won a BMI award, and was ranked Number 2 on the Billboard charts. Cliff played a part in forming the Academy of Country Music, and was one of the first members of the board of directors. He was nominated for both Vocalist of the Year and Bass Player of the Year in 1968.

Cliff's contribution to the birth of the Bakersfield Sound is difficult to put into words. He was there in 1949 with the innovators. His vocal style and musicianship were an inspiration to the other musicians, and his personality helped draw crowds that would help the sound grow. It would take another chapter to list all of the artists who have recorded his songs, and many of them made movie scores. His music and songs covered several music categories, from pop to jazz and country. At one point or another, Cliff worked alongside all of the stars who made Bakersfield famous.

Cliff is a member of the Bakersfield Country Music Museum, has items on exhibit there, and performs there at fundraising events. Cliff still writes and has his own home studio. Cliff lives in Ontario, California with his wife Maxine. They suffered the loss of their son David after a long illness on January 5, 2009. They have two granddaughters, Danielle and Davelle, and six great grandchildren, Kristin, Samantha, Jamie, Mandy, Trevor, and Madeline.

Afterword: Cliff's Death

Some of the hardest lines I will write in this book are about the death of my longtime best friend, Cliff Crofford. Cliff and I did a show in Bakersfield for the Bakersfield Country Music Museum, of which we are both charter members. He enjoyed a great performance, doing some of his hit songs. He was in good voice and great spirits and the crowd was so appreciative.

Shortly after that show, Cliff suffered a stroke and passed away two days later on November 22, 2009. Many of his longtime friends came to his service to say goodbye to a true friend. I miss him very much as I put this book together, and wish I could share some stories with him. I use this chapter to say a last goodbye to my good and loyal friend.

THE BUCK STOPS HERE—
BUCK OWENS

The Owens family owned a mule named Buck, and when Alvis Edgar Owens Jr. was about 4 years old, he announced to his family, "from now on, call me Buck." And so it was. "Buck" Owens was born August 12, 1929 in Sherman Texas to Alvis Edgar Sr. and Maicie Azel Owens. Maicie was a tough woman with the desire to raise her children well and to teach them to be strong, productive, and have a strong Christian faith. They were sharecroppers in northern Texas, not far from the Oklahoma border.

This was the Dust Bowl era, and the beginning of the Great Depression, and things were tough all over. Along with farming his own acres, Alvis Edgar Sr. would also hire out, working with other dairy farmers and milking early mornings and late evenings. As the dust storms continued blowing the topsoil away, farmers were talking of giving up, and word had it that they would find a better way of life by heading west. Thousands of folks were leaving Texas, Oklahoma, Kansas, and other Midwest areas in pickup trucks loaded top to bottom with all their belongings.

Buck said there were ten folks in the old Ford when they left Texas in 1937, five adults and five children. The trip took several days since they were pulling a heavy trailer his father had built for the trip. They would stop at night and camp alongside the road, sleeping on mattresses and cots they carried with them. The thousands of people were on the road west were looked down upon by the locals, who felt threatened and worried that they would lose their jobs to the travelers. They would even warn their kids to stay away from the labor camps.

The Owens family didn't make it to California. They broke down in Phoenix, Arizona. They had family in Mesa, Arizona, so they took what they had and made a home there. Buck's father found a job as a laborer, hired himself out as a truck driver, and did dairy work. Buck said they had no running water, so his father would tie a 30-gallon barrel to the car and fill it at a local well. It was a tough life.

When harvest came, the Owens family drove to California and saw Bakersfield and the San Joaquin Valley for the first time. They lived a nomad existence, moving up and down the valley, working for whatever crop was in season. They traveled back and forth between California and Arizona, with Arizona being their home base. Buck never forgot those days, and after he began playing in clubs in the San Joaquin, he would see some of these field workers and have compassion for them. In his office in Bakersfield, he had this large poster of a woman dressed in fox hunting clothes standing beside a beautiful and classy Rolls

Royce. The poster read, "Poverty Sucks." Buck knew this to be the truth.

When he was still very young, Buck's folks bought him a mandolin and a guitar, the very instruments that would lead him from the fields to the honky-tonks. Buck said even if the honky-tonks would not let him in, he would hang around the back door and listen to the sounds. His father cautioned him to stay away, saying, "Nothing good ever happened in a honky-tonk," and reminded Buck that he had been baptized in a river in Chandler.

As Buck practiced his music, people would tell him that he was a good singer, but he wanted to be known as a guitar player. So, he bought himself a steel guitar. In Mesa, he met a man named Mac MacAtee, who hired Buck as the steel player in his band "Mac's Skillet Lickers." It was there that Buck met a young singer named Martin Robertson, who later changed his name to Marty Robbins. He also met a young girl singer named Bonnie Campbell out of Blanchard, Oklahoma.

Still just teenagers, Buck and Bonnie were married in 1948. They soon welcomed their first son named, "Buddy" Alan, and less than a year later, their second son, Michael, was born. Buck would work at night in the honky-tonks, then in the morning, he would go out and pick oranges or cotton. He had some trouble staying in and keeping his jobs because he was so young.

Soon Buck and his family made the move to Bakersfield, where there was more country music and more bars than in Mesa. When she first arrived in Bakersfield, Bonnie took a job as a waitress at The

Clover Club. Buck came later and made the rounds, checking out the nightclubs, watching, learning, and thinking about how he could fit in. Buck and Bonnie had separated by then, but they loved both of their sons and shared their concerns about the future. Buck found a job at The Round Up that offered four guys $40 per night. That was only $10 each take-home pay.

Buck played with his signature honky-tonk attitude even then. Bill Woods heard about Buck's playing, and went to see him. He later told me, "I hired him immediately after I heard him play."

In 1951 Buck went to work at the Blackboard. He worked there for seven years, developing his craft and meeting influential people like Ferlin Husky, who would teach him about style and trademark sounds. He was introduced to the recording world, and would travel with Woods, Ferlin, and later, Tommy Collins. During this time, he met Ken Nelson, a producer at Capitol Records in Hollywood who would play a big part in Buck's life a few years later.

Buck's job at The Blackboard was to play the telecaster guitar, and he loved it. The crowds and many pickers came to watch and listen. One night, the regular singer didn't show up, and Bill Woods told Buck he wanted him to sing. Buck didn't want to, but he had been hired to work. Bill said he wanted to sing in the Jim Reeves manner, lower register, but Bill advised, "I would change keys going up," and it worked. Buck's voice cut through all the noise and chatter, and carried to all the parts of the big room.

It was at this point that Buck met Harlan Howard, a songwriter living in the Los Angeles area who would come up with Wynn Stewart and try to sell his songs. Harlan would come up on weekends. He and Buck would hang out, leave the club around 2:00 a.m., go to Buck's place, and write songs until daylight.

The Blackboard Club in Bakersfield and the Palomino Club in Los Angeles were two of the most popular clubs on the West Coast. Stars would work the Palomino Club, then go to Bakersfield to the Blackboard, and Buck worked with all of these stars, from Ernest Tubb to the Everly Brothers to Patsy Cline.

When country music came to television in Bakersfield, Buck was one of the first sidemen picked. He appeared with Jimmy Thomason on "The Louise and Jimmy Thomason Show" on KBAK TV. He also made appearances on Herb Henson's "The Trading Post Show."

Buck recorded some on Tally Records. Everyone was trying rock tunes at the time, and he recorded his now-famous "Hot Dog" during the mid-fifties under the name "Corky." He recorded some things with Bakersfield Records. He later signed with Capitol Records, and even though he had become a big star in Bakersfield, his first record with Capitol did not sell.

Buck took a job with his friend Dusty Rhodes in Tacoma, Washington at a radio station. In 1960, at a club called The Britannia, he met a young girl named Loretta Lynn. He said, "She comes in wearing a blue suit with white fringe with her pant legs stuck in these white boots!" She won a watch as the first place prize in a singing contest.

Another picker he met in Washington was a 15-year-old Don Rich. Though he was still too young to play in honky-tonks, Buck would take Don with him when he played dance halls. When he drove to Los Angeles to record, Don went along with him. On the way down, Don said later, "Buck was driving, I was playing guitar, Buck was singing, and I would sing harmony with him." Buck would say, "He sounded like me, we could read each other's minds." Buck worked with Don on the guitar, teaching him country licks. The birth of the Bakersfield Sound was now in full swing, though no one realized it yet.

In 1960, Buck's song "Under Your Spell Again" hit the Top 10. Buck returned to Bakersfield, and Don followed not far behind. Buck set up his home base at the Fresno Barn.

One Friday night, I was doing two shows at Doc's Club in Bakersfield. Before the first show was over, Buck quietly walked into the club, and we talked between shows. Buck asked me to front for his band and be his bandleader. I turned my band over to my brother and joined the Buck Owens Show, soon to be known as The Buckaroos.

We began at the Fresno Barn. The band members were myself on vocals and guitar, Bonnie Owens on vocals, Voni Morrison on vocals, Jay McDonald on steel guitar, Wayne Stone on drums, and Don Rich, 19 years old at the time, on lead. We would book country stars to appear when Buck would be out of town visiting radio stations, promoting his records or making appearances. He received no loans or any other financial help from the label, so he financed this all on his own. We in the band raised the money for his travel, promotion, and living expenses.

When Buck was home, we would do package shows with folks like Roger Miller, Rose and Cal Maddox, Bobby Bare, Wynn Stewart, and many other stars of the day. We would travel the 110-mile ride from Bakersfield to Fresno, Don and Bonnie would ride with me, and Buck and his wife Phyllis would follow us. After the show, we would always stop at a restaurant in Kingsburg, California for breakfast. Most of the time Don and I would have a hot beef sandwich or a big bowl of chili with a hundred crackers. These were happy times.

Buck never liked big introductions. Even on "Hee Haw" it was always a simple, "Here's Buck Owens" or "Here's Roy Clark." I recall a time when we were in Pismo Beach, California opening a show for Hank Snow. We were at The Rose Garden, and the place was packed. Even though Snow was the closing act, it was clear that this was Buck's crowd. Don said of Buck, "You need to give the chief a big introduction tonight."

We laughed about it, knowing Buck wouldn't like the idea. We opened the show, did three numbers, and I was going to say, "Folks, put your hands together for the fastest rising star in country music." I was only able to get out "Folks, put your hands together..." before Buck ran out and was there by my side as I continued, "... for the fastest man in country music." Don and I were laughing so hard we had trouble getting into Buck's first number.

We had a very pleasant and motivated group. We all saw country music being reinvented, but didn't realize it was part of the birth of the Bakersfield Sound. We talked about it over the years, and Buck said, "I was just doing what I wanted to do."

Bonnie Owens, who saw it all unfolding and worked alongside us, was married to both Buck and later Merle Haggard, said, "We were just working hard to come up with the best songs we could."

Buck was a man who worked for his fans, and he expected the best effort from the band. We were expected to be on time and ready to work with a positive attitude, no drinking, no smoking on stage, always wearing a smile and being friendly with the fans. Buck did not drink, and neither did I. I ran the band the way he would, and his wife Phyllis was great at handling the ticket office and financial part of the band. When Buck was out of town on the road, things continued smoothly in his absence.

By the early sixties, Buck was doing more dates on the road, often taking Don with him. Buck's success was based on obvious talent, but it also came from hard work, lots of self-confidence, and the ability to make friends. One of these friends was all-night disc jockey on WSM in Nashville, Ralph Emery, who would become a fan and a lifelong friend to Buck. Ralph was instrumental in making Buck an international star and bringing attention to the Bakersfield Sound.

Buck was certainly a self-made man, and self-educated in many ways. He had a silent but strong business sense about him. I grew up with some of the same desires, wanting to be in music. In school, I studied business and tax law, and took training in accounting and special tax courses. When Buck and I would travel together, or if I was visiting them at home in '60 or '61, we would often talk tax issues. He wanted to know about depreciation and deductions he could take on the road. We seldom talked songs. I was writing at that time for Patsy Cline. He would ask me from time to time to write him a song, which I never did, something I regret to this day.

Buck's business attention was always evident in his ability to hire talent. He expected loyalty and people's best effort in their work, and he was always quick to reward them for that effort. One such story he liked to relate was a surprise he had for six of his staff members at a barbecue. He called them forward, thanked them for their service, and handed them each a package with $5,000 in cash inside. He found it a real joy to watch their reactions when they opened their paper bundles.

Red Simpson once told me about a time when he was touring with Buck in the early sixties. Buck was about to go on stage, and the two of them had been sitting together. When Buck got up, he handed Red a brown satchel bag, and told him to watch it closely for him. Red said he was hungry, so he set the satchel down on the bleachers and went to get himself a hot dog. After returning to bleachers, he decided he was still hungry, so he went and got another one. After

Buck came off the stage, Buck said, "Red, hand me that satchel." He opened it and inside were stacks of money, somewhere between $10,000 and $20,000 cash.

Buck's one and only manager was Jack McFadden. Jack was hired on a handshake and remained Buck's manager until the day of his death, more than thirty years later. In 1964, Buck and McFadden formed OMAC Booking Agency. It would handle folks like Joe and Rose Lee Maphis, Wynn Stewart, Merle Haggard, Freddie Hart, and Rose Maddox. He also formed Blue Book Music Publishing with Harlan Howard, and when Harlan moved to Nashville, Buck bought him out. In 1980, he sold the company to Tree (now part of Sony/ATV). Buck purchased the radio station KUZZ in Bakersfield and acquired two award-winning radio stations in Arizona that were sold just a few years ago. He also bought his sister Dorothy's television station KDOB TV, later to become KUZZ TV, along with other business ventures in Bakersfield in November of 1989.

Buck joined Dwight Yoakam in 1988 after meeting him on a show at the fairgrounds in Bakersfield. Dwight had called on Buck and asked him to sing a couple of songs with him. Merle Haggard was to be on the show, marking the first time Buck and Merle had played together in 25 years. A few months later, Buck teamed up with Dwight to record a song Buck had in his catalog called "Streets of Bakersfield" written by Homer Joy. This song brought him his last Number 1 record and pulled him out of retirement for a while and he toured some with Yoakam.

For years, the city of Bakersfield received requests to name a street after Buck, an idea that embarrassed him throughout the '70s and '80s. In the spring of 1995, it was brought up again in a Rotary meeting, this time by Ray Mish. He talked to his fellow Rotarians about waiting too long to honor their celebrity, and they agreed to change the name of Pierce Road to Buck Owens Boulevard.

Buck made his mark on the Bakersfield map in another way as well. When he learned that Caltrans was going to demolish the yellow arched "Bakersfield" sign that had for fifty years spanned Highway 99, he took action. He bought the sign for one dollar and made plans to move it to the corner of Buck Owens Boulevard and Select Avenue. Portions of the sign still stand there today beside the Crystal Palace.

Buck opened the Crystal Palace in 1996 at an estimated cost of $10 million. It contains a bar, a restaurant, a dance area with concert seating, and a country museum with displays of Buck's guitars, clothing, and many photos of his life experiences and friends. The entrance has a bronze statue of Buck and some of his friends. Country stars are always stopping by for concert appearances.

All of Buck's family is involved in the business. His nephew, Mel Owens, runs Buck Owens Productions. The Buckaroos are kept busy with their duties at the Crystal Palace as the house band. Jim Shaw, the keyboardist, is the right hand man, and he deals with catalog matters, leasing videos, material, etc. Terry Christoffersen, the lead guitar and steel player, works in the research department. Bass player Doyle Curtsinger is print manager for the publication business.

In the '90s, Buck had some serious health problems. He had surgery on his throat and tongue, followed by a stroke. He bounced back and kept his spirit and vitality, and kept building his ever-increasing empire.

Buck would tell anyone that his achievements far exceeded his dreams. Between 1962 and 1967, he recorded nineteen consecutive Number 1 songs. In 1964, he recorded two songs on the same record that reached Number 1, "My Heart Skips a Beat" and "Together Again." In the charts, he went on to have five more reach the top spot and twenty-six others hit the Top 10. He received twenty-eight BMI awards for his radio singles. He performed at Carnegie Hall, co-hosted the television series "Hee Haw" for seventeen years, which can still be seen today on TV reruns, and was inducted into both the Nashville Songwriters Hall of Fame and the Country Music Hall of Fame in 1996.

Buck was one of the first recording artists to own his own masters, and he encouraged others to do the same when in a position to do so. In August 2007, the Fort Worth Star Telegram published its opinion of the top 100 songs. "Crying Time," written by Buck and recorded by Ray Charles, was rated Number 10. "Act Naturally," written by Johnny Russell and Voni Morrison and recorded by Buck, was rated Number 48. "Together Again," written and recorded by Buck, was rated Number 68. The Bakersfield Sound pioneers were represented well, as Merle Haggard had three songs on the list, and Dallas Frazier had one.

His ability to overcome the health problems and build the Crystal Palace is a monument to Buck, his career, and his Buckaroos. Buck Owens passed away from heart failure in his sleep on March 25, 2006 at his home outside Bakersfield at the age of 76. He is survived by three sons, "Buddy" Alan Edgar, Michael Lynn, and Johnny Dale; his seven grandchildren, Paul, Doug, Amy, Jennifer, Brent, Demi, and Corbet; and his three great-grandchildren, Macy, Jake, and Hailee. He is also survived by his nephews Mel Owens Jr., Keith, and Larry; his nieces Sandra, Nita, Rae Jean, and Kim; and millions of fans and friends.

His viewing was held on April 1st, 2006 at the Crystal Palace, and his funeral services were held at the Valley Baptist Church, 4800 Fruitvale Ave. in Bakersfield on April 2, 2006. The large church was filled to capacity with special seating for the overflowing crowd. Many music celebrities attended, and his long-time friends Herb Pedersen and Chris Hillman performed. Larry Daniels, his long-time friend and former employee at his stations in Arizona, provided the eulogy. Mel Owens Jr., John Berry, John Owens, Buddy Owens, Mike Owens, Dwight Yoakam, Trace Adkins, and Lulu Roman all played a role as well. Pastor Roger Spradin delivered the message. Radio and television stations from around the nation filled the parking lots. My wife, Ruth, and I were there to witness the incredible amount of love and respect shown from around the country for Buck Owens.

Buck's contribution to the birth of the Bakersfield Sound is nearly impossible to define. It dates to the fifties, when Bakersfield country music came into its own with the song "A Dear John Letter." Tommy Collins' "You Better Not Do That" brought the spotlight to Bakersfield. Buck was part of that, playing guitar for Tommy and creating a guitar part on his telecaster that was truly Bakersfield. I saw and heard Buck creating his own sound, not knowing it would later come to be known as the Bakersfield Sound. Although it cannot be put into words, in truth Buck gave the sound a voice to audiences both domestic and international.

The legacy of Buck Owens lives on at his Crystal Palace. His son Buddy, along with the Buckaroos, still play the Palace and keep his songs and memory alive.

THE QUEEN OF THE SAN JOAQUIN—BONNIE OWENS

Bonnie Campbell was born in 1929 in Blanchard, Oklahoma, to Wallace and Davis Campbell, one of eight children. Her family, like many others in the Dust Bowl days, came west looking for a better way of life and settled in the Mesa, Arizona area.

Bonnie first met Alvis Edgar "Buck" Owens in 1945 at the Malona Roller Rink in Mesa. They were both teenagers. He played guitar and that was what sparked her interest in him. They began dating, spending time around the roller rink and going to the movies. Buck had a non-paying, 15-minute show called "Buck and Britt" at a Mesa radio station that co-starred Theryl Ray Britten. Little Bonnie Campbell showed up there one day, and Buck asked, "What are you doing here?"

Thinking she had come to watch him, he was surprised when she said, "I'm singing." He didn't even know she could sing. In 1947, Buck helped Bonnie get a job with Mac MacAtee and the Skillet Lickers.

In 1948, Bonnie and Buck were married. Their oldest son "Buddy" Alan Edgar was born shortly after, and their second son, Michael Lynn, was born in 1950. Bonnie stayed home, looking after the children and the house, and Buck would play music at night in the local clubs then get up the next morning to go out and pick oranges.

In 1951 they were beginning to have marital problems, so Bonnie and the boys headed for Bakersfield where Buck's uncle Vernon and his wife Lucille lived. Buck followed before long and set out looking for clubs to find a job. He met up with steel player Dusty Rhodes at this time. Finding work was harder for Bonnie, but she found a job as a car hop at a hamburger place at Union and Truxtun Avenue, and she sat in sometimes at the Clover Club to do a few songs with Fuzzy Owen and Lewis Talley. Bonnie and Buck remained separated for a while before they could afford a divorce, but they stayed cordial with each other for the sake of the boys.

Therman Billings, the owner of the Clover Club, was a customer at the drive-in where Bonnie worked, and he and his wife got to talking with her one day. They asked if she would be interested in becoming a cocktail waitress. She said yes, and the singing waitress began her career at the Clover Club. Billings told her, "Anytime you want to sing, you can get up and sing." So once or twice a night or by special request, she would do just that. Bonnie's sister, Betty Bryand, was a waitress at the Blackboard at this time, and on her nights off, Bonnie would sing with Bill Woods at the Blackboard. Her name was starting to be known around town.

At this time, Bill Woods and Rita Goodwin recorded a Hillbilly Barton song called "Dear John Letter." Bonnie and Fuzzy Owen decided to record it as well, with Bonnie doing the singing and Fuzzy doing the narration. Both recordings of the song received a lot of local attention. Ferlin Husky and Jean Shepard went on to record the song for Capitol Records, and it went to Number 1 in all the national country charts and became a big part of putting Bakersfield on the country music map.

In 1953 Herb Henson, Billy Mize, and Bill Woods began a TV show called "The Trading Post Show." A few months later, most of the musicians at the Clover Club joined the show as the house band, which included Fuzzy Owen, Lewis Talley, Roy Nichols, and Bonnie. Bonnie was dating Fuzzy at this time. They were singing duets, and even recorded some on the Mar-Vel label with Fuzzy's band, the Sun Valley Boys. They were drawing big crowds while making appearances throughout the Valley with the Trading Post Gang. In the summers, they would go to the park in Kingsburg, California for a huge gathering. Bonnie and Fuzzy recorded a song on Tally Records which drew a lot of local attention called "Just Between the Two of Us."

One night in '61, Bonnie saw a young man who seemed somewhat familiar. She had watched him a few years back when Lefty Frizzell called him on stage at Rainbow Gardens. She introduced herself, but it was some time later before they got to know each other. His name was Merle Haggard.

Though they were now divorced, Bonnie and Buck were professionals and they still toured some together. Their sons were their mutual concern, and both showed love for them. It was during this time that I began working as a member of the Buck Owens Show. We were working 100 miles north of Bakersfield at the Fresno Barn in Fresno, California, and Bonnie and Don Rich would ride with me. Sometimes if Buck took Don with him on a trip, I would hire Jack Collier to play guitar. One night Jack and Bonnie were talking about a man named Merle who had stopped in the Blackboard. Bill Woods had him sing a couple songs and was impressed by his voice.

We worked together for two years, Bonnie all the time working on songs, making notes while we were driving or over breakfast, and always thinking of a melody or a lyric. We never wrote together. Most of the time, we were too busy driving. The weather in the mighty San Joaquin is something else, especially at 2 or 3 in the morning. Forging our way through heavy rains, dense fog on Highway 99, and trucks all over the road, it was difficult to write songs.

Bonnie also continued her part-time work at the Blackboard. When we were not with Buck, she worked on her writing. She had chances to meet the many stars coming through Bakersfield who stopped by "The Trading Post Show" or the Blackboard, and she developed friendships that would pay off years later. She did not get to know Merle Haggard much until Al Brumley booked him on Cousin Herb's show.

Later, Fuzzy Owen became Merle Haggard's manager, and he suggested that Bonnie and Merle record "Just Between the Two of Us" in 1964 on Tally Records. They did, and it was a hit that spent 26 weeks on the charts. Shortly afterwards, Ken Nelson took notice of this, and with Fuzzy's encouragement, Merle was signed to a contract with Capitol Records.

Bonnie left for a tour of Alaska. Merle was having serious trouble in his marriage, his four children were with his mother, and he was unhappy. He was missing his singing partner. He flew to Seattle, called Bonnie about him coming over and finding work for himself in Alaska. Bonnie did not agree at first, but eventually she gave in. The rest, as they say, is history. A few weeks later, they were married. Bonnie had been dating Fuzzy almost from the time she had moved to Bakersfield, and though Fuzzy was taken by surprise, Merle and Bonnie never looked back.

They began focusing on Merle's career. Bonnie had been married to Buck, dated Fuzzy for a long time, then married Merle, and they all worked together. Merle signed with a booking agency owned by Buck Owens and Jack McFadden, so these relations seemingly caused little problems for them.

Bonnie continued to write. Her life with Merle brought on a lot of responsibilities, taking care of kids, the household, looking out for the band members, looking after Merle, and doing recordings and rehearsals. She always carried pen and paper, and as Merle would come up with song ideas, Bonnie was there to write them down. Sometimes she would get writer's credit. She served as a critic on a tune she received an award for, "Today I Started Loving You Again." The award was for over one million plays, and is one of my favorite songs of the Haggard catalogue.

Bonnie tells it that she and Merle were better friends than they were a married couple. She would say, "I was more of a sister, even to the band." Bonnie and

Merle separated in 1975 and were divorced in 1978. She later married Fred McMillan and moved to Missouri, but she continued to work professionally with Merle. She would fly out of Springfield, where Haggard's tour would take off from, and ride the tour bus from place to place.

Bonnie's career was spread out over many years. She had six solo albums, two duet albums with Haggard, two gospel albums, and dozens of recordings singing backup for Merle. In the late '90s, she joined Kathy Robertson in recording two CDs for which all proceeds would go to Roy Nichols, who was ill at the time.

Bonnie left Merle Haggard's band after over 30 years when she began suffering from Alzheimer's disease. She passed away on April 24, 2006 in Bakersfield, California at the age of 76, after having been ill for some time.

Bonnie's father and mother, her brothers Charley and Delmer, and sisters Lucille and Jean preceded her in death. Bonnie was survived by her sisters Betty, Gail and Loretta; her son Buddy and his wife Katy, her son Michael and his wife Kristin; six grandchildren, Paul, Doug and his wife Brandy, Amy and her husband Shawn, Corbet, Brent, Jen and her husband Scott; and three great-grandchildren, Macy, Jake and Hailee. She is also survived by numerous nieces, nephews, and cousins, and a world of fans and friends.

My wife, Ruth, and I attended her funeral, just short of one month after Buck's funeral. We felt and prayed for Buddy and Michael, losing both parents in such a short time. The service was officiated by

Pastor Roger Spradin, the same pastor who officiated at Buck's service, and the eulogy was presented by Kristin Owens, Bonnie's daughter-in-law. There was an overflowing crowd that included many musicians she had worked with over the years, her best friends, Fuzzy and Phyllis Owen, and many friends and fans that will miss her always.

Bonnie could laugh at her position in life, being married to two of the biggest stars in country music and divorcing each of them but remaining best friends. Bonnie's contributions to the birth of the Bakersfield Sound are too numerous to mention in full. Her positive outlook and winning smile would light up most days and recording sessions, and will be remembered by all who were lucky enough to see her on tour. Her professionalism, her contribution to song writing, and her dedication to the recording sessions were all important to the artists doing creative work.

MR. PERSISTENT—
FUZZY OWEN

Fuzzy Owen was born in Conway, Arkansas in April 1929. At twenty years of age, he was headed west, ready for the world with no idea what the future held in store for him. With the turmoil between North and South Korea, every young man was caught up in this problem. It was difficult to get into college or find a career because of the draft.

Fuzzy picked cotton during the day with his cousin Lewis Talley and would play music three nights a week at The Blackboard Café. At that time, it was a small café with an actual black board where customers could write messages to a friend, or an employer could leave a message if he needed help in the fields. Fuzzy played steel guitar, Lewis played rhythm guitar, and they performed songs of the Earnest Tubb Era. Later on, they played in Springville for a short time with The Sons of the Ryaneers, and this is where I first heard them since I was living in Delano, a town close to Springville and Porterville.

In 1950, it was off to the Army for Fuzzy. After serving two years, Fuzzy returned to Bakersfield, and he and Lewis picked up where they left off in their music careers. Before long, they took up residence at the Clover Club in Bakersfield.

Fuzzy was a musician, but he was also interested in the business end of things. That interest was further nurtured in 1953 when he and Lewis came across a song written by Hillbilly Barton called "Dear John Letter." Two different recordings were made of the song. He and Lewis Talley printed a hundred copies of "Dear John Letter" for radio, and both recordings of the song drew a lot of attention. Fuzzy and Lewis felt good about the song and could see some potential. They made a deal with Barton, who did not own a car at the time, and traded a 1947 Kaiser Automobile to Barton in exchange for the song.

Ferlin Husky, then known as Terry Preston, was working in town as a disc jockey and had a band at The Rainbow Gardens. A young singer from Visalia, California was also in town working with Bill Woods. Her name was Jean Shepard, and she had recently signed with Capitol Records and recorded "Crying Steel Guitar Waltz." Bill Woods told the story that they all went down to Capitol Records and talked to Ken Nelson about recording "A Dear John Letter." Nelson turned down the song, saying it was a war song and there was no war going on, but they told him how the song was doing on a local level and that interest was still growing. Ferlin was recording with Capitol, as was Shepard, and it was finally agreed that Shepard would do the singing and Husky would do the narration. They recorded the song later in 1953, and it quickly went to Number 1 on all the national country charts.

Ferlin used his real name on this record. This event was a huge part of the birth of the Bakersfield Sound.

In the late fifties, Lewis Talley and Fuzzy Owen started Tally Records. Both entered the publishing world as well, with Talley's Lu-Tal Publishing and Fuzzy's Owen Publishing. Soon they moved to a small room on Baker Street where they made several recordings on a one-track recorder. In 1956, they recorded a rock and roll tune called "Kathleen" by Wally Louis. They leased the recording to another company for distribution, and it reached Number 15 on the rock charts. They later moved the studio to Talley's House on Hazel Street.

Fuzzy had a wide presence in country music. Besides his nightclub work at the Clover Club, he joined Cousin Herb on TV's "The Trading Post Show." He, Bonnie Owens, Al Brumley Jr., Roy Nichols, Jelly Sanders, and Johnny Cuviello were popular stars on the show in the mid-fifties. They worked nights at the club and days at the recording studio, which closed two or three years later after Lewis and his wife divorced and the house was sold. Fuzzy also toured in the early days with Buck Owens, and made some of the early national TV appearances on shows like "The Jimmy Dean Show."

In 1961, Fuzzy met a young Merle Haggard when Merle returned to Bakersfield after a stay of two years and nine months in San Quentin on a burglary charge. Johnny Barnett Sr. had hired Merle at The Lucky Spot to fill in on his two nights off. Jelly Sanders was heading the band there, often included Red Simpson on piano, and occasionally Fuzzy would play along with Merle.

Fuzzy liked Merle's singing and decided to take a closer look. Merle could do it all, country, rock, blues or whatever was offered to him. Fuzzy convinced him to record for Tally Records. A recording engineer in Bakersfield, Ed Smizer, made a makeshift studio and recorded Merle on a tape machine and a small mixing board. Merle sang one of his songs, "Skid Row" and one of Fuzzy's songs, "Singing My Heart Out." They traveled to Phoenix to work on the tapes. They were excited about the outcome, and on their way back to Bakersfield, they stopped by Cliff Crofford's house in Ontario to share their excitement. Cliff said, "My record player was of such poor quality, Fuzzy said, 'Give me that record and put it away.'" Nevertheless, they made 200 copies for radio stations, and that was the beginning of a career for Merle Haggard.

By 1964, Capitol had big plans for Merle. Fuzzy sold Merle's Tally Catalog to Capitol and became Merle's full-time manager. In 1965, Merle formed a band and named it The Strangers after his first top of the charts release, "All My Friends Are Gonna Be Strangers."

Fuzzy and Merle were off and running. Lewis Talley was a part of the team, and so was their bus driver. Lewis passed away in 1986 at age fifty-eight. Fuzzy is still active in the management of Merle Haggard, a relationship that has continued for over forty years. Fuzzy has helped guide Merle's career, and seen the "country poet from Bakersfield" be inducted into the Country Music Hall of Fame, Song Writers Hall of Fame, and receive countless other awards and nominations.

Fuzzy still makes his home in Bakersfield with his wife Phyllis. His contribution to the birth of the Bakersfield Sound has been huge. He was involved from the beginning in its surge and growth, and he worked with all of the major players, most notably and extensively with Merle Haggard.

THE PARTY· BOY—
LEWIS TALLEY

Arkansas-born Lewis Talley had his fingerprints on many parts of the birth of the Bakersfield Sound. Lewis, known as Louie to his friends, and his cousin, Fuzzy Owen, first came to Bakersfield in the late forties fresh out of high school. One of their first jobs was at the small Blackboard Café where they would play music on the weekends. Their sound then was a very popular Earnest Tubb honky-tonk sound, with George French on accordion, Fuzzy on steel guitar and Louie on rhythm guitar and vocals.

They later played a short time in Springville, California with the Sons of the Ryaneers before both were drafted to a two-year term in the Army. Lewis was the first to enter, and when he and Fuzzy returned to Bakersfield in 1952, they picked up music right where they had left off.

In 1953, they recorded a song on Mar-Vel Records called "A Dear John Letter," written by Hillbilly Barton. Rita Goodwin recorded the vocals, Bill Woods did the narration and fiddle, and Lewis was on guitar. The record received a lot of local radio play, but Mar-Vel had no distribution, so it made few sales.

Lewis liked the song and the idea of trying to market it, so he and Fuzzy began talking a deal with Barton on the song. Lewis was a persistent risk taker, and was reluctant to give up on his ideas, so it came as no great surprise when he offered Barton a 1947 Kaiser auto in exchange for his song. Barton took the deal.

A young Bonnie Owens also recorded "A Dear John Letter," with Fuzzy Owen doing the narration. Both recordings received a lot of local interest, both on radio and from personal appearances. Talley and Owens were high on the song and believed it could be a hit. They took Bill Woods, who was friends with the Capitol Records folks, and Ferlin Husky down to Hollywood to try to convince Capitol's Ken Nelson to record the song. Woods said that they debated for a long time. Nelson was not high on girl singers. Through a combination of Louie's persistence and Bill Woods' salesmanship, Nelson finally gave in.

Jean Shepard and Ferlin Husky, both Capitol artists, recorded "Dear John Letter" with Jean singing lead and Ferlin doing the narration. It became a huge hit, a Number 1 song on Billboard and Cashbox, and every radio station in the country. Capitol sold over one and a half million records, proving a girl could sell records, and that a good story can always sell, in times of war and in times of peace. The song went so big that Barton pressed for some ownership of it.

Shepard and Husky became major stars and moved to Nashville. They had one more hit, a sequel called "Forgive Me John," this time writer credits going to Shepard and Hillbilly Barton though the sequel was written by Ferlin Husky for Jean. This recording brought attention to Bakersfield and shed a spotlight on other Bakersfield artists to follow.

In the late fifties, Lewis Talley and Roy Nichols were fixtures at the Porthole Club in Ridgecrest. They were very popular there. Sometimes when they were booked elsewhere, Lewis would call me to fill in for him. I was there firsthand to see just how popular they were, and I would hear stories of their after-hours activities. Louie was always ready for a party, and always dressed the part in his stage clothes designed by Turk. When Hollywood was looking for someone to play the part of Hank Williams in the movie, "Your Cheatin' Heart," it was reported that Louie was in line to audition for the part, as he lived a similar lifestyle to Hank Williams. When the time came for the screen test, Lewis was out living up to his name, so the studio picked George Hamilton, who had no country music background at all.

In 1955, Lewis started a label called Tally Records and a publishing company called Lu Tal publishing. One of the first artists to record with Tally Records was Buck Owens with a rockabilly song called "Hot Dog." Buck recorded under the name Corky Jones, not wanting to give up his hopes for a country career, something George Jones did as well with Starday Records, recording a rockabilly song under the name Thumper Jones.

They only stayed at that location for a couple months before moving to Baker Street. The landlord was Saba's Men's Store, and their start-up equipment was a one-track tape machine and a three-channel mixing board. The new location was small, but in 1956 they recorded a song there called "Kathleen" by a rock and roll artist named Wally Louis. They leased the song and distribution out to a company, and it reached Number 15 on the pop charts in 1957.

Soon Lewis bought a house on Hazel Street and they moved the studio to that address. They built a unit on the back, and Lewis and his wife lived in front. The studio had the same equipment, but now had an echo chamber in the form of a bathroom. Many Bakersfield musicians recorded at this location well into the sixties. It was a place to learn and experiment in sounds and recording techniques. These ideas that would be a huge benefit to Lewis and Fuzzy in their future producing efforts, as they would go on to produce several Number 1 songs for Merle Haggard. They had such faith that they would one day find the talent and the material, and both were inspired to keep investing in the process.

Talley and Owen met Merle Haggard in 1961, after he had served a stretch in San Quentin. They had heard some of his work before he had left for prison, and thought he had some promise. Merle was now sometimes playing in Johnny Barnett's band at the Lucky Spot, where Fuzzy Owen and several other musicians would fill in for Johnny. Fuzzy liked the smooth sounds of Merle, and convinced him to record for Tally Records.

Lewis was helpful to the career of a very young Merle Haggard. Once Merle called him looking for a one-night-a-week job. Lewis said, "I can get you a week if you want." They drove over the mountains toward Ridgecrest, California in Talley's white El Dorado. Lewis had many connections in the music industry, and they found Haggard a job at Paul's Cocktail Lounge in Tehachapi on Friday and Saturday nights.

In 1962, Haggard recorded his song "Skid Row" for Tally Records. He also recorded one of Fuzzy's songs, "Singing my Heart Out," and other songs like "Sing Me a Sad Song," "Just between the Two of Us," a duet with Bonnie Owens, and "All My Friends Are Gonna Be Strangers." A recording engineer by the name of Ed Smizer helped with the production of "Skid Row" with a tape machine and a three-channel amp that worked as a mixing board. They made 200 copies for radio. It got radio's attention, and eventually Capitol Records', which was their intention from the beginning. They finally sold Haggard's Tally catalog to Capitol in 1964.

In the mid-sixties, Lewis and Fuzzy were working with Merle Haggard, recording him on Tally Records, looking for that big break-out song. They found some chart success with "Sad Song," which had Lewis, Fuzzy, and Bonnie Owens working nights, mailing out records to DJs around the country. They also recorded a song by Merle and Red Simpson called "You Don't Have Very Far to Go," which had a Tommy Collins song called "Sam Hill" on the B side.

But Lewis and Fuzzy were still looking for their career song, and found it when they visited the home of Liz Anderson, mother of Lynn Anderson. She sang and played several songs, and they were all pleased and surprised at the material they were listening to. The song they had been looking for was called "From Now On, All My Friends Are Going to Be Strangers," which would go on to become Merle's first Top Ten record in 1965.

Fuzzy became Merle's manager and helped him get ready to go on the road. Merle hired his band and named them The Strangers after his first big hit. Lewis was there from the very beginning, and stayed with the group the rest of his life, serving in whatever capacity was needed, whether it be producer, bus driver, friend, or party participant. It made no difference to him, as long as he was there.

Lewis Talley was living with his mother on Lake Street in Bakersfield when he passed away of a heart attack in 1986 at age fifty-eight. His contribution to the birth of the Bakersfield Sound is deep and wide. At one time or another, he touched the lives of all those who played a part in the music being created at that time. He will long be remembered by the fans and musicians of Bakersfield.

THE COUSIN—HERB HENSON

Herbert Lester Henson was born May 17, 1925 in East St. Louis, Illinois. He came to California during World War II, after leaving the navy on a medical discharge. Like a lot of the musicians of this era, his first jobs were agricultural, working in the cotton fields in the San Joaquin. But this sales-minded people-lover was not going to do much hard labor. Herb found a job playing piano six nights per week at the Wagon Wheel on Ninth Street in Modesto. He met a local disc jockey there named Chester Smith, who went on to gain national fame for himself. This was the same place he would later discover Del Reeves as well.

Herb moved on to Fresno, where he met Bill Woods. Herb was working a recorder at a small music store. Soldiers would come in, and Herb would play background on the piano while the soldiers sent messages home to their family. Bill recalled, "He played church-style music, and wanted to learn honky tonk. We got acquainted, and I hired him for some jobs." Woods talked to Herb about Bakersfield, about the radio stations and the club scene, all of which were buzzing at that time. Minter Field was in full operation with the training of fighter pilots during World War II, and entertainment was in high demand. It wasn't long before Herb was on his way to Bakersfield.

Sometime later, Herb told a story on his television show about his move to Bakersfield. He rented a trailer and put all of his possessions in it. As he was driving down Highway 99, he looked back and saw the trailer was on fire. He jumped out of his car, unhitched the trailer and watched it burn with all of his things. As he dug through the ashes, the only thing he found that was not burned was a picture of Bill Woods.

In Bakersfield, Herb landed a part-time job on station KMPC and took a job with Ted Salsbury Cleaners going door to door to pick up laundry. He said if he saw a piano in the living room, he would start a conversation about it, play some gospel tune, and end up picking up additional clothing. Herb did stints as a comedian, and musician at many dance halls and honky-tonks like the Blackboard, Clover Club, and the Rainbow Gardens. Henson had the gift of gab and could sell anything. His success on radio as a popular disc jockey made his move to KERO TV a fairly easy sell, especially since Jimmy Thomason had already begun his country music show on KBAK TV a week or so earlier.

In September 1953, the general manager of KERO gave the okay for Herb's TV show. It would be called Cousin Herb's "The Trading Post Show." The cast was made up of Herb's mentor, Bill Woods, Billy Mize on steel guitar, Johnny Cuviello on drums, a young Carlton Ellis, and starred the most popular piano player in Bakersfield at the time, Cousin Herb Henson.

Herb had recorded the Arlie Duff song "Y'all Come." It gained some national airplay and was a local hit. Herb, always the salesman, used this as the theme for the show. Herb was always himself in the show, and never set himself up as the star. He was the pitch man, the sales man, and always the funny man. He had this likeable way about him, and though he could be serious in a business deal, Herb was a friend to all and was loved by all. The show was a huge hit right from the start.

Herb had great success with the performers he hired for the show, and he always had something for viewers of all ages. He hired Carlton Ellis and Dallas Frazier when they were both teenagers. Dallas wore a bandana around his neck, something he picked up from Ferlin Husky, and he used it to keep time while singing. It became his trademark, and adults and young people both loved it.

Herb did well when he hired Roy Nichols. The music took on a different quality when Roy joined, and the show increased in popularity even more. Herb's hiring of Al Brumley Jr. was also a real winner. Al was the son of Albert Brumley Sr., the great gospel writer, and Al Jr. could handle the gospel songs. He was also young and handsome, and had a Marty Robbins-type voice. Al would later take on the roll of producer.

In 1961, a call came into Brumley's office saying his brother-in-law was a singer, and the caller spoke so highly, Brumley agreed to an audition. The young man walked into Brumley's office, picked up his Martin guitar, and Brumley would later say, "From the first note, I knew he was a winner." The young man's name was Merle Haggard. He was hired for two nights per week. When fan mail started coming in, he was hired for five nights per week.

Many country artists were involved in the show throughout the years it ran. Almost every star of that time would visit the show at one point or another, from Ernie Ford to Johnny Cash, from Spade Cooley to Gene Autry, Lawrence Welk, and everyone in between. Several local artists, like Buck Owens, Chester Smith, and a very young Barbara Mandrel, also appeared on the show. The cast eventually expanded to include Bonnie Owens and Fuzzy Owen as well.

"The Trading Post Show" was a wide-reaching success. On spring and summer weekends, Herb and his Trading Post Gang could go to Hart Park and draw as many as 5,000 to 10,000 fans. They could do the same at a park in Kingsburg, California, and they could fill any hall around. KERO was a clear channel station with a signal that reached well beyond Fresno, so they could book shows outside Bakersfield, advertise on air, and have a sellout.

All this time "The Trading Post Show" was going head-to-head with "The Jimmy and Louise Thomason Show" on KBAK and both were doing well. They were different enough from each other that the TV audience wanted to see it all. But Thomason quit his show in June of 1954 to run for the state senate against Senator Jesse Dorsey. He did not win the election, but his wife Louise finished out their remaining two-month contract, then they moved back to Waco, Texas to began a show on WACO TV called "Home Folks Show." By default, Henson won the ratings battle.

Herb was a natural for a live TV show, and even his commercials were part of the entertainment. He may have had a TV ad copy in front of him, but he was off on his own, ad-libbing all the way. Even he did not know what he was going to say next. I saw him walk outside of the studio where we were doing the show to do a used car pitch for Leo Meek, his main sponsor, and the wind was blowing so hard. He would stay, with hair and clothes blowing every which way, but that became part of the show, rain or shine.

Herb had many requests for appearances that he could not make. He would often call on me, as I had the Valley Rhythm Boys and could travel easily. Sometimes I would go on the show to promote an event in the early '60s. My brother Johnny played bass on the show for a while.

In the late 1960s, Cousin Herb accepted a management job for the radio station KUZZ. The station had been started in 1959 when a radio man out of Delano, Bob Scott, had taken over a small rhythm and blues station in Bakersfield, call letters KIKK. Scott and I had talked about the need for a full-time country radio station. Overnight, we did exactly that with KIKK. Eventually the call letters were changed to KUZZ, as a cousin to the other pop stations in town. In the late '60s, Scott got into a management dispute and left the station, and Cousin Herb was offered the management position. So, now he had more responsibility and more publicity to go along with it.

On September 12, 1963 at the civic auditorium in Bakersfield, twenty-four different artists gathered to honor and celebrate Herb's 10-year anniversary with KERO. Stuart Hamblen, Glen Campbell, Roy Clark, Buck Owens, Tommy Collins, Merle Haggard, and many others performed. Ken Nelson was there to record the show for rebroadcast. No one realized that this would be the last big show for Herb Henson.

On November 26, 1963, Herb finished the afternoon show and went home. His wife Katherine was away bowling with the KUZZ bowling team. Herb had gone for a walk, a routine prescribed by his doctor, and was heading over to his sister's house. A short time later, there was a knock on the door at the Henson home. Someone needed to use the telephone. Cousin Herb was lying in the street.

Herb and Katherine's four sons were still young, and were taken to their aunt and uncle's house to shield them from the news. The television was announcing bulletins every few minutes that Cousin Herb had died of a heart attack only four days after the assassination of President Kennedy. Cousin Herb Henson was dead at age thirty-eight. He left behind his wife Katherine and his four sons Rick, Keith "Dusty", Mike, and Kenneth "Rusty." Rick and Dusty live in Bakersfield, Mike now lives in Oklahoma, and Rusty lives in Ashland, Oregon.

Herb Henson gave eyes and ears to the Bakersfield Sound, and a direction for it to form. He helped keep an audience to support the clubs and musicians so they might continue to experiment. Herb's death left a void on TV. There has never been another show matching

Cousin Herb and "The Trading Post Show." The local folks will long remember him and still like to talk about things he would say and do on the show. Herb is honored in the Bakersfield Country Music Museum exhibits at the Kern County Museum.

THE TEACHER—
FERLIN HUSKY

Ferlin Husky was born in Missouri in 1925 and came to California in his early twenties. His first contact with Bakersfield was a chance meeting with Bill Woods in 1949. Woods was at the Buckaroo Bar in Salinas, California one day where Ferlin, who was going by the name Terry Preston at the time, just happened to be singing in the back room. Bill asked to see him, and they spent some time together. Bill told Ferlin about how music was developing in Bakersfield. Ferlin was young, but very driven, talented, creative, and full of self-confidence, the perfect combination for a budding recording artist.

Ferlin spent some time with Four Star Music Recording under the name of Terry Preston, sleeping upstairs in the Four Star offices. He had some radio success during this time, but not much.

About a year after their first meeting, Bill Woods was working as a DJ at KBIS. He wanted Ferlin to come to Bakersfield, so he told the manager of KBIS, Hal Brown, about Ferlin's talents, and asked about a DJ position for Ferlin. Brown said, "If he is as good as you say, and can sell a solid one-hour show, I will give him one." Woods called Ferlin to Bakersfield, and in two days' time, they had sold the show completely. Ferlin's DJ work was a success from the start.

Ferlin became host to an amateur show alongside Bill Woods at the Rainbow Gardens on Friday and Saturday nights that was also broadcast on KBIS. Ferlin's band was called The Termites, and was made up of Bakersfield sidemen. Rainbow Gardens was a large dance hall on Union Avenue that would hold a crowd. It had no seating except a bench around the walls of the ballroom, and the place was always packed for their shows. Folks would gather and stand in front of the bandstand for a close-up look at the performers. Admission was $2, a high price in those days. Most of the musicians who played a part in Bakersfield made appearances there, like Fuzzy Owen, Cousin Herb Henson, Lewis Talley, Oscar Whittington, and Tommy Hays.

One night at the Gardens, Ferlin hired a young man named Leonard Sipes. Leonard ended up moving into the upstairs bedroom of Ferlin's house, and he began performing regularly at Rainbow Gardens with Ferlin and The Termites. In 1954, Ferlin introduced Leonard to Ken Nelson of Capitol Records and Cliffie Stone, the publisher for Central Songs. Cliffie signed Leonard as a writer for his company. Ferlin continued to work with Leonard on his style and stage presence and encouraged his writing. Ferlin gave him the name "Tommy Collins."

Another find for Ferlin was Dallas Frazier, a 12- or 13-year-old who entered and won the talent contest at the Gardens. The crowd loved him. Ferlin took him on, supported him, taught him, and helped him move in with Tommy Collins. Dallas would go on to reach the top as a songwriter.

Ferlin also spent some time in the early fifties at the Blackboard Café in Bakersfield, where he met Buck Owens. Ferlin helped Buck develop his craft, assisting him in establishing a trademark sound, and Ferlin's influence can be heard in the guitar parts Buck did on Tommy Collins' recordings for Capitol.

Ferlin's big breakthrough came in 1953 with the song "Dear John Letter." Jean Shepard sang, and Ferlin did the narration. It was a smash hit that went all the way to the top of the charts. Both Ferlin and Jean became national stars, and the Bakersfield Sound began to spread in popularity. Sometime later, the two of them did a sequel to "Dear John Letter" called "Forgive Me John," and it was another huge hit.

Ferlin had given up the name Terry Preston and now recorded using his given name, Ferlin Husky. He went on to a great career, going to Nashville with songs like "Since You're Gone," "I Feel Better All Over More Than Anywhere Else," "Wings of a Dove," and other hits. He starred in several movies and TV shows, and did his "Simon Crum" comedy act as part of his show. In 1974, he made the charts again with a couple of his old California friends with the songs "Freckles and Polliwog Days" and "Champagne Ladies and Blue Ribbon Babies," both written by Dallas Frazier.

Ferlin Husky was one of the first people from Bakersfield to reach national recognition and acclaim.

He played a part in the birth of the Sound with his energy and his focus on style and individuality, his ability to discover talent, and his willingness to work with musicians to develop their own unique sound. For years, I thought Ferlin should be in the Country Music Hall of Fame for all that he has accomplished in his career, and at last he was inducted in 2010. Ferlin still performs some, and made his home on a ranch in Missouri until his death.

Afterword: Ferlin's Death

I was so happy to learn Ferlin was inducted into the Country Music Hall of Fame in 2010, and shocked to learn of his passing on March 17, 2011. I knew he had been ill, but was sad to learn of his death. I watched a rerun the following Monday of an interview on the RFD channel with Ralph Emery. Ferlin was very much himself, always full of laughter and fun. It was a bittersweet moment for me and for all of his fans.

LEONARD—TOMMY COLLINS

Tommy Collins was born Leonard Sipes in Oklahoma City, and came to Bakersfield at age twenty-one with a big desire and a clear country voice.

Leonard was struck by the music scene in Bakersfield. He attended a show at Rainbow Gardens and introduced himself to Ferlin Husky (then going by "Terry Preston"). Leonard told Ferlin that he, too, was in country music. Ferlin asked if he was good, and Leonard said, "I don't know."

Ferlin said, "You know! Tell me the truth."

Leonard said, "Well I guess so," and he was hired without audition.

Leonard ended up moving in with Ferlin, taking the upstairs bedroom. He played at the Rainbow Gardens with Ferlin and his band The Termites, and worked at a gas plant for Richfield Oil Co. Leonard would also hang out at the Blackboard with Bill Woods, soaking up any knowledge he could. He would often work the Sunday jam session with Bill Woods. It was there one Sunday afternoon he met his soon-to-be wife, Wanda Shahan. They began dating, and three weeks later, they were married in Las Vegas.

In 1954, Ferlin Husky introduced Leonard to Ken Nelson, a producer with Capitol Records, and Cliffie

Stone, who had a publishing company called Central
Songs. Stone signed Leonard as a writer, and Nelson
signed Leonard as an artist with Capitol. Nelson
mentioned that Leonard's name would not be easy to
sell. While Ferlin was recording one of Leonard's songs,
the musicians were hungry, and Leonard offered to go
get sandwiches. When one wanted a "Tom Collins
drink," Ferlin renamed Leonard "Tommy Collins."

Tommy recorded two tunes on Capitol, "You
Gotta Have a License" and "You Better Not Do That,"
with Ferlin helping on the guitar arrangement. "You
Better Not Do That" went to Number two on the
Billboard charts in 1954. Tommy was on his way, with
appearances at the Jamboree in Houston, the Ozark
Jubilee, the Red Foley Show, and the Grand Ole Opry.
Disc Jockeys voted him "most promising." Praise came
from Billboard, Downbeat magazine, and Cashbox.

Tommy was a favorite on local television and often
appeared on the Cousin Herb Show. In 1954, Herb
invited me to appear on his show, and the special guest
was Tommy Collins. It was my first appearance on TV,
and I was a nervous wreck. Tommy really stole the show.

On a swing through Texas in 1955, Tommy's
promoter had him following a kid from Tupelo that
Collins had never heard of. Andy Griffith was the
headliner, and the kid from Tupelo was Elvis Presley.
No one knew much about Elvis, Collins said, but they
all knew him after a show in Jacksonville, Florida at
a baseball stadium. Andy Griffith and Collins were
standing in the dugout, watching as fans fought to

get on stage with Elvis. Collins recalled, "That was a breakout show for Elvis." Griffith said, "It's an orgy."

A short time later, Collins became a Christian at the Central Baptist church in Bakersfield, and not long after he felt a calling to preach. Ken Nelson and his wife June tried to talk him out of quitting country music, but failed. Tommy was discouraged with the music business. Elvis' success was controlling the charts in '57 and '58, and fiddles and steel guitars were disappearing from country music. A lot of country artists were trying to do rock or rhythm and blues material in the late fifties. Tommy moved to Berkeley and attended Golden Gate Baptist Seminary from 1960 to 1962, and went on to Sacramento College in 1963.

Tommy pastored many churches, eventually becoming an interim pastor in Mettler, a community south of Bakersfield. His interest in the ministry began to dim after a while, and needing more money to support his family, he began selling Kirby vacuum cleaners. In 1964, Collins resigned the ministry, signed with Capitol Records, and began recording with Merle Haggard. Although Tommy was out of the ministry, he was still called on for special counseling, and he was always there to lend an ear to anyone in need.

I remember seeing him at the civic auditorium in Bakersfield, where twenty-four entertainers gathered to honor Herb Henson's 10-year run with KERO TV. He had appeared with folks like Glen Campbell, Stuart Hamblen, Roy Clark, Buck Owens, and many others on the show. Henson had been ill for some time, and he had requested that Tommy officiate his funeral if the worst should happen. When Henson passed away a short time later in 1963 at age thirty-eight, Tommy did just that.

Tommy's return to Capitol was not a big success, so he signed with Columbia and began to record in Nashville. He found the recording routine much different now and had a hard time keeping the Buck Owens telecaster sound going on his recordings. He did hire Fred Carter, who played a Fender telecaster, but Nashville still had a different idea on recording.

Buck Owens called Tommy Collins and said he would like to do an album of Tommy's songs on Capitol. Several of the songs featured Buck's playing. The album had 12 songs, including "High on the Hilltop" and "If You Ain't Lovin' You Ain't Livin.'"

In 1964, Buck invited Tommy to join the Buck Owens Tour, a package-type show that included Merle Haggard and Rose Maddox. Tommy opened all the shows, but he overslept after a show in Minnesota. The bus left for Iowa without him, and he had to hitch a ride from a disc jockey. Tommy confronted Buck, asked for his check, and went home. On his way back to Bakersfield, someone mentioned a new TV show Buck would be joining. That show was called "Hee Haw." This was all poor timing for Tommy.

Tommy had some success with his song "If You Can't Bite, Don't Growl," but he developed a drinking problem during all the traveling, and his last session with Columbia was in 1968. His marriage also ended around this time. After his divorce, Tommy would later say, "I didn't care much what happened."

In 1976, he moved to Nashville for good, and tried repeatedly to get off drugs and alcohol. He says, "I finally saw the light that if I didn't stop I would kill myself," and he did get himself together.

I saw Tommy in the late '80s when a lot of Bakersfield musicians gathered to celebrate the start of a country music museum in Bakersfield. They had a show one evening to honor Bill Woods, and many people, myself included, were part of the show. Tommy did a set singing some of the hits he had early in his career, such as "High on the Hilltop." The Bakersfield Californian snapped a picture of him exiting the stage, and put it in the next morning's paper. I purchased a paper early in the morning and took it to where I was meeting Tommy and Al Brumley Jr. for breakfast. They had arrived before me, and I could see beside Tommy a big stack of newspapers. I walked in, and Tommy said "How are things going?" I told him, "The reason I'm late is I've been all over town looking for the newspaper, and they've all sold out!" They had a big laugh, and Tommy joked he would sell me one.

Tommy's achievements were very dear to him. He wrote over 300 songs, twenty-seven of them recorded by Merle Haggard, including "The Roots of My Raisin' Run Deep." He won several BMI awards for songs through the years for such songs as "You Better Not Do That" in 1954, "Whatcha Gonna Do Now" in 1955, "Carolyn" in 1972, and "The Roots of My Raising" in 1977. Tommy got his Platinum record in 1987 when George Straight's album "Ocean Front Property" with Tommy's song "Second Chances" sold its millionth copy. He is part of the Bakersfield Country Music Museum, and has an exhibit there. He was inducted into the Songwriters Hall of Fame in 1999.

Though Tommy did not preach anymore, he was still a Baptist deacon. He attended church with his old roommate and friend from Bakersfield, Dallas Frazier. He had three grown children of his own and two adopted daughters. He made calls to aid and comfort parishioners, and officiated the wedding ceremony of his old friend Merle Haggard in 1993. Tommy was remarried in August of 1998 to Hazel, and they lived happily on his one-acre ranch. Tommy passed away from complications due to emphysema on March 14, 2000 in Ashland City, Tennessee, having been proudly sober since 1982.

Tommy Collins was among the first artists from Bakersfield to reach national stardom. His contribution to the birth of the Bakersfield Sound is in the area of hope and inspiration to the locals, a lesson in style, a lesson in arrangement, and an inspiration in song writing. Bakersfield was proud to call him its own.

PHOTOGRAPHS

Bakersfield Record Stars

Bill Woods, Lawton Jiles

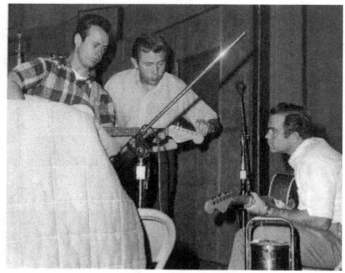

Don Rich, Buck Owens, Red Simpson; Capitol Recording Session

Jerry Hobbs and Eugene Moles, Sr.

Herb Henson

Joe and Rose Lee Maphis and their two children

Lawton Jiles and Buck Owens

Lawton Jiles and Red Simpson

Lawton Jiles and Tommy Hays

Lawton Jiles, Cliffie Stone, and Buster Beam

Lucky Spot (after the fire)

Merle Haggard, Snuff Garrett, Cliff Crofford, and Fuzzy Owen

Snuff Garrett, Cliff Crofford, and Walter Brennan

Tommy Duncan and Tex Ritter; Western Jamboree Poster

Trading Post Gang

Wynn Steward

Valley Rhythm Boys

The Blackboard Cafe

Lawton Jiles

Lawton Jiles and Larry Daniels

Tommy Collins, Lawton Jiles, and Larry Petree

Lawton Jiles and Johnny Cuviello

Bonnie Owens, Lawton Jiles, Ruth Jiles, and Inez Savage

"BAKERSFIELD RECORDING COMPANY"
COUNTRY - RHYTHM & BLUES - POP.

November 8,1958

Mr Lawton Jiles
PO Box 284
Delano, Calif

Dear Lawton:

Will you please sign the enclosed contracts. Return
both copies to us and we will finish processing and return one
to you.

Please note that the contract is retroactively dated
back to the date of original contract.

If you have any questions , please call us.

Yours truly,

BAKERSFIELD RECORD CO

BILL WOODS   JOHNNY LUVIELLO   CHRIS CHRISTINE

A Cherished Gift from Buck Owens

Engraving on Pickguard

Buck Owens note

THE GRAND LADY OF THE GRAND OLE OPRY— JEAN SHEPARD

Though she was born Ollie Imogene Shepard in Pauls Valley, Oklahoma in 1933, she would become known in country music as Jean Shepard. "Don't call me Jeannie," she'd say. Her large family found it hard to make a living during the Great Depression, so they migrated to central California and settled in the Visalia area, a farm area rich in cotton, fruit and vegetables. Though young and small, Jean hit the cotton fields and helped the family any way she could. Her family was filled with musicians, and Jean was gifted with a strong voice. In 1948, while Jean was in high school, she began her professional career playing bass fiddle in an all-girl band.

A few months later, Hank Thompson was in the Tulare area. Jean was sitting in on a song with The Brazos Valley Boys, and Hank caught the show. He was impressed, and asked Jean if she wanted a career in country music. Even though there were not many girls in the business at the time, Hank mentioned her to Ken Nelson, A & R man at Capitol Records. Ken was not high on girl singers at the time, so he did not call.

A year or so later Thompson was in the area again, and Jean went to see his show. Thompson remembered Jean, asked what happened with Capitol, and Jean told him that she had never heard anything. This time Hank called and personally asked for an audition interview. In 1952, after the huge success of Kitty Wells' "It Wasn't God Who Made Honky Tonk Angels," a Hank Thompson song, Jean received an audition and a Capitol contract.

Jean's first session had to be something special. She was tuned in to country music, knew all the songs being played on the radio, and DJs worked to keep everyone informed of not only the artist, but the best musicians of the day. Jean recorded four songs on her first session, with band members Jimmy Bryant, Speedy West, Cliffie Stone and Billy Strange, all great musicians and producers in their day. Jean's first single was "Crying Steel Guitar Waltz," which came out in 1952. Although it did not chart, it received a great deal of airplay and served notice that there was a new girl in town.

Then in 1953, Capitol was debating whether to record a Hillbilly Barton song titled "A Dear John Letter." It was finally agreed that Jean would sing the lead, and Ferlin Husky would do the narration, as both of them were Capitol artists at the time. Even after all of the hesitation surrounding the song, it became a smash hit. No one could turn on the radio without hearing it. Jean and Ferlin had both served their time in country music, and now, after their whirlwind success, became national stars. As Jean was not yet twenty-one, her parents signed a special order that Husky would be responsible for her welfare, and they toured the country together.

Jean experienced much success in the years that followed. She and Ferlin recorded a sequel to "A Dear John Letter" called "Forgive Me John," written by Ferlin Husky for Jean. It went on to become another very popular song. In 1955, Jean joined the Red Foley Ozark Jubilee, where she found the song "Satisfied Mind," which became her first solo single to reach the Top 10. Other Top 10 songs of hers were "Beautiful Life" and "I Thought of You." Jean Shepard and Cliff Crofford were the first country folks to be on George Day's early afternoon variety show on KERO TV. In 1956, Jean was invited to join the Grand Ole Opry, and remained a member for over fifty years. She also continued to record and tour. In 1959, Jean was voted Cashbox Magazine's Top Female Artist.

In 1960, Jean married Opry star Hawkshaw Hawkins. In 1963, while pregnant with their child, she received the unfortunate news that Hawkshaw had been killed in a plane crash with their friends Cowboy Copas, Patsy Cline and manager Randy Hughes. Some years later, she married Benny Birchfield, a well-known figure in country music.

The sixties found Jean still recording for Capitol, with songs like "Second Fiddle to an Old Guitar" and "A Tear Dropped By." She also had some success with a duet with Ray Pillow called "I'll Take the Dog." She had many Top 10 songs, and many middle of the chart songs.

In 1973, she left Capitol to join United Artist Records. Her first single was a Bill Anderson song called "Slippin' Away," which peaked at Number 4 on the Billboard chart. A special tribute to Jean and Bakersfield came when Jean was elected to the Country Music Hall of Fame in 2011.

Jean's contribution to the birth of the Sound came in the beginning. She got her start in the San Joaquin Valley, and moved up to work closely with the Bakersfield pioneers like Bill Woods, Lewis Talley, Fuzzy Owen, and Ferlin Husky. She helped by laying the foundation with the recording of "A Dear John Letter," a song that brought national attention to Bakersfield. The Sound was in its infancy, but it kindled a fire in the country folks of Bakersfield. In the words of Bonnie Owens, "We knew we were on the right path." Bakersfield will forever be proud of Jean Shepard and her contribution to the birth of the Bakersfield Sound.

THE DISCOVERY—
DALLAS FRAZIER

Dallas Frazier was born October 27, 1939 in Spiro, Oklahoma, and was raised in and around Bakersfield. Dallas was twelve years old when he discovered Ferlin Husky on a Bakersfield radio station, where Ferlin was working as a disc jockey and going by the name Terry Preston at the time. Ferlin was also playing music on the weekends and for special events with his band, The Termites. He was holding a talent show at the Rainbow Gardens Dance Hall, south of Bakersfield on Union Highway. When Dallas heard about the contest, he was determined to enter.

On a Saturday night in 1952, 12-year-old Dallas introduced himself. The good looking, skinny kid walked up to the microphone with his personality in high gear and belted out a little Jimmy Dickins tune. It got the attention of the whole crowd, including Ferlin Husky.

Dallas discovered Ferlin, then Ferlin discovered Dallas, marking a moment in time that would cement a lifelong relationship. After Dallas' performance at the Rainbow Gardens, Ferlin and his friend Bill Woods went searching to learn more about him. They found that Dallas' father and mother were divorced. His father worked on a Greenfield ranch in an area south of Bakersfield, and his mother was living with relatives in McFarland. Dallas had no transportation for making appearances in Bakersfield.

Ferlin arranged for Dallas to stay with him and his wife Betty, rooming with Tommy Collins, another discovery of Ferlin's. Ferlin hired Dallas to become a member of the Termite band. Tommy Collins was still very young as well, and now Ferlin had two young termites to watch over, groom, and guide into a career in country music. Tommy worked with Dallas, showing him his first chords on the guitar he had purchased for $10. The relationship that started then would last a lifetime. Tommy and Dallas would both move to Nashville in later years, just a few minutes away from each other, and they attended the same church.

When Dallas was thirteen, Ferlin introduced him to Ken Nelson, an A & R man for Capitol Records. Nelson agreed to audition Dallas, but Nelson read a newspaper during the audition, and at the end said, "Not now, maybe later." When the following year rolled around, the time was right. At fourteen years of age, Dallas recorded "Ain't You Had No Bringing Up At All" and "Love Life At Fourteen" on Capital Records.

A short time later, Dallas went to work on Cousin Herb Henson's TV show, a 45-minute show that aired six days a week. Dallas was a livewire on the show. He wore a bandana around his neck, and pulled it back and forth in a seesaw fashion to keep time, a trick he learned from Ferlin Husky. That bandana became a trademark for him, and the audience loved it. He was with the show for about four years. After Ferlin left for Nashville, Dallas lived with Cousin Herb's family for a time. At 18, Dallas married his girlfriend, Sharon Capani.

Dallas became a member of the Cliffie Stone Show in Los Angeles, "The Home Town Jamboree," joining folks like Tennessee Ernie Ford, Tommy Sands, Molly Bee, Gino Quinn, Speedy West, and other local stars. He worked this show until it went off the air four years later.

In 1959, Dallas hit the big time as a songwriter with "Alley Oop," a novelty tune that climbed all the charts. The song was recorded by three different groups, and the Hollywood Argyles' recording reaching Number 1 on the pop charts.

The fast lane was not comfortable for Dallas, and he began to withdraw from the music scene and turn to his church. He moved to Phoenix, then back to McFarland. He wrote some music and produced a few records, but he soon stopped again and moved to Portland, Oregon where he lived quietly from 1961 to 1963.

Ferlin came through Portland on a tour some time later. The two friends got together, and Ferlin asked Dallas to write for him and his publishing company again. Still young and full of song ideas, Dallas decided to try again. He and Sharon moved to Nashville and began what would become a very creative time in his career.

Dallas enjoyed much success in his writing. He also became a recording artist, releasing songs like "Tell It

Like It Is" and "My Baby Packed Up My Mind and Left Me". In 1964, Dallas wrote a blockbuster song called, "There Goes My Everything," recorded by Jack Green in 1966. It was later recorded by Englebert Humperdink, Don Cherry, and Elvis Presley. "There Goes My Everything" is said to have been recorded more than a hundred times. In 1966, Dallas wrote "Elvira," which went on to be a huge hit for the Oak Ridge Boys. He also wrote "Aint Had No Lovin'," which went on to become a top 10 song for Connie Smith, and "I'm a People," which became a big hit for George Jones.

Dallas became one of the most sought after songwriters in Nashville with recordings by Willie Nelson, Brenda Lee, Merle Haggard, Moe Bandy, Rodney Crowell, Charley Pride, Ronnie Hawkins, Randy Travis, George Straight, Emmy Lou Harris, Patty Loveless, The Oak Ridge Boys and more.

In 1988, Dallas again grew tired of the stress in the music business and retired, wanting to work in the ministry along with his longtime friend, Tommy Collins. It is rumored that he is now returning to the songwriting world for the third time, but says this time he will be careful to do it his way and write the way he feels. "I know I have some things left to say," he says.

Dallas Frazier is remembered fondly in Bakersfield, and has won countless awards. His contributions to the birth of the Bakersfield Sound are huge. He contributed to the fan base, drawing crowds and attention to the music, giving the opportunity for other artists to develop their talent. Dallas' songs and his performances had the Bakersfield feel to them with that good time, honky-tonk attitude. Dallas should one day be in the Country Music Hall of Fame. He will always remain in the hearts of the Bakersfield fans who remember him so fondly after all these years.

SUITCASE SIMPSON—
RED SIMPSON

Red Simpson was born on March 6, 1984 in Hagley, Arizona. About his town, he says, "I think they had a general store and a service station. We didn't even have a town drunk; everyone just took a turn." Red was the last of twelve children in the Simpson family, which relocated to a government camp in Shafter, California in 1937. Two years later, they moved to Arvin, a town just outside of Bakersfield. They lived on Padre Street and later moved to Cottonwood Road, where Red went to school and was raised.

Red was always interested in music. His father played the banjo, and his older brother, Buster, played guitar and upright bass with Bill Woods and other bands in town in the late forties. His sisters, Lois and Ella, played rhythm guitar, and would sing songs with harmony parts like "Beautiful Brown Eyes" and "You Are My Sunshine." Red says, "I loved those sounds." About every four years, his grandfather, a fiddle player, would come out to California for a visit, and the family would all play music together.

"I would grab a broom and walk around and pretend I was playing guitar," Red recalls, "My brother Buster was playing in Los Angeles then, so he would come up. We had linoleum floors, so they would move all the furniture out of the front room and sprinkle some corn meal on the floor. Buster would bring in a couple of guitar players, and we would play and dance the night away. I was right there with my broom, and I knew some pretty good chords on the broom, and I never broke a straw."

Red got his first guitar when he was 11 years old. He had traded a bicycle for it. Red jokes, "I couldn't ride the bicycle, so I had to learn to play guitar." People around at the time tell how they can remember Red coming down Padre Street, before it was paved, on a stick horse with an old guitar on his back, singing cowboy songs he had heard in a cowboy western. "I would take my guitar and play for the class. They loved it. I would take my guitar on the bus and sing for the kids. I had more friends than you could believe," says Red.

Red remembers, "I used to shine shoes out at the Rhythm Rancho. There were musicians there like Oscar Whittington, Bill Woods, Tommy Hays, and Jimmy Jeffries. I would go out and have these guys show me chords. I could learn about one chord a night. Tuning was a problem at first, but Buster kind of helped me, but he didn't want to mess with me much. I was a dumb old kid that didn't know anything. I had a brother-in-law, James Lambert, who was married to my sister Ella who knew four or five chords and was helpful. After I was with Capitol and had several records out, he would tell everyone who would listen, 'I taught that little bastard everything he knows about the guitar.'"

Red guitar playing was influenced by Bill Woods and Roy Nichols. Some years later, Red would get to play with Roy and Wynn Stewart in Las Vegas at the Lariot Club. Red learned a lot from Bill, and the two became good friends.

On radio and in the movies, Earnest Tubb, Red Foley, T. Texas Tyler, Floyd Tillman, Jimmy Wakely, Bob Wills, Roy Acuff, Roy Rogers, Gene Autry, and Sunset Carson all greatly influenced Red Simpson. Red was around age twelve when the Maddox Brothers and Rose would come to the Rainbow Gardens. "I was always there as close as I could get to watch Roy Nichols on guitar," he reflects. "These two guys gave me the want-to." Red also enjoyed the showmanship and flashy clothes of the Maddox Brothers and Rose. For Red, it was all about the show business.

When Red was young and still shining shoes out at Rhythm Rancho, Bill Woods and the guys would let Red get up and sing sometimes. Bill also spent some time helping Red learn to play the piano. When fans would put money in the "kitty" at the Rhythm Rancho, Red would have to split it with the band. "Sometimes I would make four dollars," Red recalls. "It was better than shining shoes."

Red had a story of one of the earlier times that Tex Ritter was a guest star at the Rhythm Rancho. After Tex finished his set and was walking toward the front, Red was standing by the door. "Mr. Ritter would you like a shine?" the young Red said.

Mr. Ritter answered, "Yeah, why not? Come on out here to my car." Tex walked out to the side of the club, where a black chauffer opened the car door for Tex, and he sat down. Red put his shoeshine box on the ground, and Tex put his boot on it. There was a dim light by the side of the building, so Red couldn't see all that well, but he went to work, and thought he did a good job.

So he said, "How's that, Mr. Ritter?"

Tex looked down and said, "Son, I think you have ruined my favorite pair of boots. They were green, and I think you have painted them black." He grabbed Red by his hair and Red started crying. Tex turned Red loose, and away he ran. "Boy, you come back here!" Tex yelled.

Red recalls, "I thought he was gonna bust my britches, but I went back. Ol' Tex handed me a dollar and said it was a pretty good shine anyway." Red would be reminded of that incident years later when he ran into Tex again before Tex moved to Nashville to become part of the Opry. Tex was appearing at the Clover Club and needed a ride to the airport, so the bandleader asked Red to take Tex to the airport. Red had an old car with the head liner torn out. On the way to the airport, Tex asked, "What kind of car is this taxi?" Years after that, after Red had some records out and was appearing for the last time on the Grand Ole Opry, Tex was the master of ceremonies. Before he brought Red out, Tex said, "I'm sure glad the boy's recording now, because he sure can't shine shoes!"

As a teenager, Red worked as a swamper, carrying tools for Buster and his other brother, Bill, in their house plastering business. Even though he could never please his older brother, Buster was still his hero. One time, after they were headed home from a hard day,

Buster stopped the truck at a big grape vineyard and said, "Red, let's get some grapes." So they picked some Thompson Seedless grapes, and Red said, "Boy, these are good." Buster replied, "Yeah, they taste better when you steal them." With a laugh, Red remembers his brother saying to him when he was about fifteen, "Red, keep working on your music. When you are twenty-one, we will start a band." The band never happened. Buster left a short time later for Pocatello, Idaho, and joined a band there.

Red's life, like so many other up-and-coming talents, took a turn with the Korean War. Red joined the Navy and was off to Korea in January 1952. Red had developed more than a passing interest in the piano ever since, as a child, he and his sister would play a neighbor's old upright piano. In the navy, he served on the USS Repose, which was a hospital ship. There was a piano in the bottom section of the ship near the morgue, so Red spent all his spare time down there practicing without a disturbance from anyone. Three or four guys there played music, so they formed a band, and called themselves the Repose Ramblers. They had a steel lap guitarist, a rhythm player, stand-up bassist, an accordion player, and Red on lead guitar. This was his first band. He recalls taking all of his instruments to the top deck on the nights when there was no movie showing, practicing fiddle, guitar, and mandolin.

I asked him if he ever tried to write during this time. He said, "A little, but not much." Bill Woods recalled a song Red wrote when he was thirteen or fourteen years old. Red went out to the chicken pen to write a song and came back with "Chicken House Boogie." This was mentioned once in a newspaper article, and at a recent appearance at a senior function, a senior citizen kept coming up to Red and asking for the "Chicken House Boogie." Red said, "Sorry, I can't remember that song, man."

I first met Red Simpson in 1954 when we entered a four-week amateur contest with a weekly winner at the Rainbow Garden put on by Bill Woods on Saturday nights. The four winners would meet again for a final at the big park in Kingsburg, California, where each Sunday during the summer Cousin Herb Henson and the Tradin' Post Gang would appear. Red had his sailor uniform on and he was having a good time. He was around twenty years old, beer in hand and surrounded by four or five girls. Eight or ten of us were backstage, waiting to go on for the contest, and I introduced myself to Red. Bill Woods stopped by and asked Red to enter the contest. He was having too much fun and was reluctant, but finally agreed. He now had lipstick all over his face, and his sailor cap had red lipstick marks around the sides, but we all went on. He would have won the contest because of his talent, but he didn't take it seriously. I won the contest, as it turns out, and the $25 prize, but lost in the finals at Kingsburg four weeks later.

Red was discharged from the Navy in 1955 at twenty-one years old after having served three years and three months. Not long later, Red met and married a young lady by the name of Ellen, and together they had three children. Times were rough, and they lived in a tiny rental house. Ellen worked part time on the weekend, and Red was making $30 or $40 dollars a week. One day, a car pulled up to the house, and Bill Woods stepped out with three bags in his arms. Bill said, "I brought you some groceries." Red told him, "Man, I can't pay for anything." Woods explained, "I just wanted to help you a little bit." Red remembers this fondly and calls him "Ol' big hearted Bill."

When Red came back to Bakersfield in 1955, Bakersfield music was going strong and the jobs were all filled. Each musician protected his job, so it was hard to get in, and Red did not have club experience. He managed to land a job out in Lamont, about twenty miles outside Bakersfield at a place called the Wagon Wheel, earning five dollars a night. He also worked picking potatoes and cotton, but after two nights and one hot day, he said, "To hell with this cotton sack. If I do anymore picking, it's going to be music," and he quit just like that.

Red started going around to different clubs, sitting in wherever he could. His old friend Bill Woods was still around, helping when he could and mentioning Red's ability. Cliff Crofford, one of Bill's recruits, was looking for a guitar player, and so he called Red. The job paid $15 a night at a place called Jack's Ranch. Red remembers realizing this was the same money as three nights at the Wagon Wheel and says, "You bet Cliff Crofford gave me my first big paying job." He was working hard on piano and hung around the Clover Club with George French. George would show him chords and little runs, but soon George left for

Louisiana and turned the band over to Fuzzy Owen. Fuzzy told Red if he came in and practiced two hours a day, he would hire him six nights a week.

While doing a part-time job as a Good Humor ice cream driver, Red wrote a song called "Someone with No One to Love." One day, he drove to Buck Owens' house, and told his old friend about the song, saying, "I have this song mostly written; see what you think about it." He recorded the song on a little reel-to-reel recorder, and in 1956, The Farmer Boys recorded the song for Capitol Records. It was Red's first cut on a major label.

Red made a point of hanging around people who were really into their music. He would go into every recording session he possibly could. One of his friends and local idols was Jelly Sanders, a member of Cousin Herb's TV Show and a guy who was now in big demand as a session player. On one occasion, when Red was at the studio with Jelly, he saw Tennessee Ernie Ford recording. Red recalls, "I walked over to the window and there he was, my hero since I was a teenager, recording 'Sixteen Tons.' I just stared at him." He stared so long, the hot coffee he was holding went cold. Red says Jelly told him Tennessee Ernie Ford recorded there all the time.

Red says, "Another time, I went down with Bill Woods. He was taking Del Reeves down for an audition with Ken Nelson, the A&R Director for Capitol Records. Nelson said, 'Okay, Del, are you ready to audition?' After Del completed his audition, Mr. Nelson looked at me and said, 'Well, what about you?'"

Red said, "No, Mr. Nelson, not yet." A few years later, he was ready to reach the big time, much to the delight of his dear friend Bill Woods.

Buck Owens once took Red down with him to a session playing guitar for Tommy Sands. It was about 7 or 8 at night, and Red says he "ran into this old boy at Capitol who asked if I wanted to go to a party, so I said, 'Hell, why not?' So he took me way up in the Hollywood hills to this big house. It was Kirk Douglas' house. I walked into the house and there were all these movie stars. It was a real blast for this country boy." Red reflects, "I went back to the studio and told Buck. He said, 'Man, I should have gone with you instead of playing down here.'"

Red worked in the clubs, filling in for Buck or Bill or other sidemen when they wanted a night off or were ill. Red also continued working on his writing and carried the lyrics with him in a suitcase, earning himself the nickname Suitcase Simpson. He still has that suitcase today in his living room.

Simpson put his heart and soul into the birth of the Bakersfield Sound, singing and writing songs that drove the music forward. He wrote and co-wrote songs for Buck Owens and Merle Haggard, and was the writer of Merle Haggard's hit song "You Don't Have Very Far to Go." His record on Capitol, "Hello, I'm a Truck," hit the top spot on Cashbox in 1971. Other top-40 singles included "Roll, Truck, Roll" in 1966, "Truck Drivin' Fool" and "A Bakersfield Dozen" in 1967, "The Very Real Simpson" in 1972, and "The Best of Red Simpson" in 1995.

Red's songs have been recorded by many of country's greatest artists, including Roy Clark, Del Reeves, Connie Smith, Ferlin Husky, Charlie Walker, Dorsey Burnett, Jeannie Seely, Homer and Jethro, Don Bowman, Stoney Edwards, Dave Dudley, Junior Brown, Ron Gaither, and Dwight Yoakum. Red's songs have also been featured on many TV shows and movies. Junior Brown's recording of Red's song was the title song in the movie "Highway Patrol."

Red continues to write, with Jiles Beam Music as his publisher. He now writes songs of family and friends, such as Merle Haggard's recording of the song about Red's friend and mentor "Bill Woods of Bakersfield." Red also writes fun songs like "The Bag Lady of Bakersfield" and "Ethel's Place." His love for Bakersfield is as strong as his love for music.

Red now lives in Bakersfield with his lovely wife, Joyce. She is a songwriter herself, and his strong support partner. Red still travels for some appearances. He works one night per week at Trouts, a local nightclub and the oldest country club in Bakersfield. He still enjoys a large fan base that follows him wherever he may be appearing.

Red has certainly been a big part and maybe the heart and soul of Bakersfield music. He is a founding member of the Bakersfield Country Music Museum, with items on exhibit there at Kern County Museum.

A big honor was bestowed on Red Simpson in March of 2012. The Country Music Hall of Fame offered an exhibition and a salute to the Bakersfield Sound. Michael Gray, the museum editor and co-curator, along with the help of Mick Buck and Tim Davis, made it all happen.

Red was the headliner and the main representative of the Bakersfield Sound. Others that appeared in that Saturday night show included Dallas Frazier, Rose Lee Maphis, Don Maddox of the Maddox Brothers and Rose, Buddy Mize, and Eugene Moles Jr., with Jelly Sander's son playing a set on the drums. Jean Shepard had also been expected to attend, but was ill at the time.

This event was a huge tribute to the Bakersfield Sound and those involved, and it was well received.

THE POET—
MERLE HAGGARD

James and Flossie Haggard left Checotah, Oklahoma and came to California in 1934. James went to work as a carpenter for the Santa Fe Railroad. He bought a boxcar in Oildale, California, and they remodeled it and made it their home. Oildale was made up of Dust Bowl folks from Oklahoma, Texas, Missouri, and Arkansas, people who knew firsthand of real poverty. Though still in the middle of the Depression, the Haggard family was doing fairly well.

Merle Ronald Haggard was born on April 6, 1937, the third child in the family after Lillian and Lowell. He was raised near the railroad tracks between the Kern River and the oilfields for which Oildale was named, about a mile from Bakersfield. By the time World War II came along, he was five years old, old enough to hear all the stories about going off to fight a war. Music brought on very personal feelings in people of that time, no matter what their age.

Merle's mother was a housewife, enabling her to devote her full attention to the children. That changed when Merle's father died of a brain tumor. Merle was just nine years old. The talk that goes on around any child during these events leaves a lasting impression, as a child is compelled to listen and not able to offer opinions or make decisions.

Flossie had to become the breadwinner. She went to work as a bookkeeper, a vocation that she would maintain for the rest of her life. Merle had lost his base of ever-ready love and support, and now found himself with unsupervised time to do whatever his mind was dwelling on at the moment. For a bright young man, full of energy and the need to prove himself, the loneliness that accompanied this newfound freedom had to be overpowering at times.

He developed a music taste early on while listening to his father's Jimmy Rogers records. His father had played fiddle in Oklahoma, but stopped after he married Flossie. I can imagine that Merle felt the urge to live out some of those songs and experience the things the songs would speak of. At an early age, Merle was aware of the stars of the day, such as the Maddox Brothers and Rose, and Bob Wills and the Texas Playboys. They would appear often in Bakersfield in the late forties and fifties at the Beardsley Ballroom, which was close enough for Merle to ride his bike to listen outside of the building.

Bob Teague, who was a few years older, relayed some time later how he met Merle. Bob was walking down the street in Oildale when he heard someone strumming a guitar. Looking over a fence, he saw Merle and struck up a conversation. The two became friends, and Bob helped Merle learn to play the guitar. As teenagers, Merle and Bob hitchhiked to Big Springs,

Texas where they were hoping to see Lefty Frizzell, but Lefty had moved away long before they arrived.

When Merle was fourteen and Teague was eighteen they were in Modesto in a place called The Fun Center out on Crows Landing Road. They had been bucking hay all day, and decided to go in for a good time. They asked if they could perform, then did a few songs, and the manager asked them to play the rest of the evening, for all the beer they could drink and $5. This was Merle's first professional job.

Merle kept working on his guitar. He had discovered Roy Nichols now, and at sixteen years old, he was the envy of many young guitar players. Merle went to see Roy, knowing they were about the same age. Merle said about Roy Nichols, "You know, Roy played guitar and traveled with those guys. Hell, he didn't even have to go to school."

A big moment in Merle's early life came when he and Bob Teague went out to see Lefty Frizzell at Rainbow Gardens in the fifties. Teague had great confidence in Merle's talent, even at 16, so he found Lefty and told him, "Lefty, this guy can play almost as good as you. Can you listen to him?" Lefty answered, "Sure." He took Merle backstage, handed him his guitar, and Merle sang a couple of songs. Lefty was impressed enough to have him sing on stage, so Merle went on stage using Lefty's guitar and sang a Jimmy Rogers song. In later years, Merle and Lefty became good friends and appeared in some shows together.

Before this, I recall Merle performing at the Rainbow Gardens one night. During intermission, he was shy and reluctant as he sang some of Lefty Frizell's song "Always Late" a cappella. He was about thirteen or fourteen years old. I think his sister was with him.

Merle was restless and in a hurry to grow into manhood. He spent time in several penal institutions and carried out numerous escapes. At seventeen, he married Leona Hobbs.

As Nicholas Davidoff wrote in his "The Country of Country" in 1997, "Merle Haggard has always regarded himself as a transplanted Oklahoman." With all of the experiences he endured in his young life, his mind and heart had a story of heartbreak and sorrow to tell. He would have to be an author, a storyteller, a professor, or a songwriter, and Merle became all of these, never forgetting the past, but putting into words and music the things we all experience in a lifetime. His loneliness during his adolescent years contributed to his ability to put feeling into a song to the point that his heart and soul came through in each line of the song.

In the late fifties, Merle, now a married man and father of two children, was arrested with two friends for breaking into a small café. They were drunk. They thought it was 3:00 a.m. and the café would be closed, but it was only 10:30 p.m. and the café was still open. People in the café saw Merle crawling out of the back window with a check cashing machine and recognized him. Merle and his friends escaped, but were arrested the next day. With his background as a troubled youth, and his many escapes from other institutions, he was labeled as "incorrigible." The judge sentenced Merle to maximum security in San Quentin Prison where he served two years and nine months. He was released in 1960. In 1972, Ronald Reagan, then governor of California, expunged Merle's criminal record and granted him a full pardon. Merle never denied or tried to cover up his past. He wrote songs about much of this experience and has become living proof that a man can turn his life around.

Merle returned to Bakersfield from San Quentin a changed man. Now twenty-one years old, still married to Leona, he returned to his family and went to work for his brother. Lowell Haggard was a Bakersfield contractor who worked digging ditches.

Merle found that Bakersfield music had turned the corner from the mid-fifties rock sounds and returned to fiddles and steel guitars again. Real country music was back in style. Johnny Cash, Buck Owens, Ray Price, Tommy Collins, and Wynn Stewart were all big stars. Buck's "Under Your Spell Again" and Ferlin Husky's "Wings of a Dove" offered a young man interested in country music something to dream about.

In '61 and part of '62, Merle played in some of the local nightclubs, learning his craft. He played bass with Buck Owens for a while, and tagged the band "The Buckaroos," a name that stuck. In 1962, he went to Las Vegas to work for Wynn Stewart with his childhood idol, Roy Nichols. In 1963, Merle made a partnership with Lewis Talley and Fuzzy Owen, the owners of Tally Records. His first release on Tally was "Sing Me a Sad Song," which carried a notable influence from Wynn Stewart. Wynn was the writer and the teacher. The song reached Number 19 on the Billboard Charts. In the mid-sixties, after his third single "All My Friends Are Gonna Be Strangers" hit the Top 10 on the charts, Capitol records took notice and signed Merle Haggard to a recording contract. Merle later named his band The Strangers after his hit song.

In 1965, Merle recorded "Just between the Two of Us" with Bonnie Owens, and it went to Number 4. After that success, Bonnie left to tour Alaska. Merle's first marriage was going badly, and they filed for divorce. Merle flew to Seattle, called Bonnie, and said he would like to come up for a few of the dates. They returned to Bakersfield as a married couple. It was during this marriage that Merle's songwriting really took off. He would pick up the guitar to sound out these songs, and Bonnie would write them down. She said she was, "adding encouragement or critique; sometimes adding lines." This continued until their divorce in 1978.

Later in 1978, Merle married Leona Williams. That marriage also ended in divorce. He had a brief fourth marriage before his marriage to his current wife, Theresa. He has three children by his first wife, and two children with Theresa. Merle loves his children and his family. At times, I wonder how many children have been named after Merle. Bill Woods named one of his children Merle Haggard Woods. Merle honored another man in this fashion as well, naming his oldest son Marty after one of his heroes, Marty Robbins.

Merle's contribution to the Bakersfield Sound is immeasurable. He was no doubt born with a honky-tonk attitude, fueled by the musicians and the honky-tonks he grew up around. He must have learned early from folks like Bill Woods, Lewis Talley, Fuzzy Owen, Red Simpson and Wynn Stewart that you have to have a hard-driving sound and a good lyric to keep a crowd 'til one o'clock in the morning.

By the time Merle appeared on the scene, Buck Owens had defined and brought attention to the Bakersfield Sound. Merle brought further attention with his songs of life. Anyone who has listened to "Silver Wings" will say they can close their eyes and see the plane with sunlight dancing off the wings. They can hear the engine roar, and see the lady in the plane. They can picture the one standing behind, watching the plane fly into the sky and out of sight. This is how a writer bares his soul, and Merle was able to do that as well as anyone, much like the great Hank Williams could. This talent and self-sacrifice propelled Merle from Beer-Can Hill, from the cotton fields, from ditch digger and truck driver, to becoming "the poet of the common man."

Merle's success in music has been great. Many of his albums have gone gold, such as "Okie from Muskogee" in 1970, "The Fighting Side of Me" in 1971, "The Best of Merle Haggard" in 1974, "Big City" in 1981, "Poncho and Lefty" in 1982, and "Eleven Winners" in 1989. He has been nominated 42 times for CMA awards, and received 56 BMI citations. In 1977, he was elected to the Songwriters Hall of Fame, and in 1994, he was inducted into the Country Music Hall of Fame. He has appeared in several feature films, including "Huckleberry Finn," "Killers Three," "Bronco Billy," and "Doc Elliot." He has also appeared in such television series as "The Waltons" and "Centennial." His songs have been featured on many television and movie soundtracks. He is currently working on a movie of his life.

Merle has remained loyal to his old friends. Bonnie Owens, his ex-wife and back-up singer, stayed with the band for over thirty years until she became severely ill. Fuzzy Owen, who was instrumental in the start-up of Merle's career, is still part of the team. Lewis Talley stayed with Merle until Louie passed away, and Roy Nichols remained with him until his health failed. Norman Hamlet, the steel player, and Don Markham, the saxophone player and backup singer, have both remained in the band for forty-three years and still going strong. Biff Adams has been the drummer for forty-two years. Merle has remained close to the co-writer on many of his songs, Red Simpson, who, like Merle, is part of the soul of the Bakersfield Sound.

In 2007, Bakersfield honored Merle by changing the name of Standard Road to Merle Haggard Drive. Traveling north on Highway 99, on the north side of town first comes Buck Owens Boulevard, then a short distance further north near the airport, there is Merle Haggard Drive. It's quite a tribute to a couple of guys that put Bakersfield on the map and brought the Bakersfield Sound to the world. Their work has inspired many of today's country singers and guitar players.

On Sunday April 6, 2008, Merle was appearing at the Fender Guitar Museum in Corona, California on his 71st Birthday. Cliff Crofford, his wife Maxine and granddaughter Kristin, and my wife Ruth and I went over to spend the afternoon visiting with Fuzzy, some of the musicians, and Merle. He had his wife Theresa and two of his sons with him in the show, Noel and his youngest son Ben. Ben played a great guitar, bringing up those Roy Nichols licks. The Sound lives on in the generations that follow. It was such a great thing to see and hear. That night, Fender presented Merle with a specially made guitar. His contribution to the birth of the Bakersfield Sound is indelible, and Bakersfield is very proud of its native son.

THE PROFESSOR—
WYNN STEWART

Winford Lindsey Stewart was born on June 7, 1934 in Morrisville, Missouri to Cleo Winford and Golden Stewart. His siblings were Patty Wanderer and Beverly Mullins. Wynn's father was a sharecrop farmer in Missouri, but during World War II he moved the family to California so that he could work at the submarine base. At the end of the war, the family went back to Missouri for a short while, and then returned to Los Angeles when Wynn, whose nickname was originally spelled "Win," was fourteen years old.

Wynn began teaching himself the guitar at the age of eight. His sister Beverly recalls music being a part of Wynn's life from the beginning. As a boy, he appeared on KWTO in Springfield, Missouri, which would later become home to the Ozark Jubilee. In high school, he formed a band and began playing at clubs in Southern California, under the escort of his father. During this time he made his first recording, Eddy Arnold's song "Anytime."

Wynn graduated from Edison Park High School in Huntington Park, California in 1951 with dreams of a music career. He followed Bob Wills and Tommy Duncan on country radio, and had a strong interest in the honky-tonk sound. He often entered and won a talent show in Huntington Park hosted by Carl Moore, who went by the name of "Squeakin' Deacon," and was a DJ on KXLA. At this talent show, Wynn met the steel guitar player Ralph Mooney. Ralph became part of Wynn's band, and the two were friends for life.

Wynn knew from the start that he had to be unique to be noticed. He was always a stylist, studying arrangements and hooks. In 1954, at age twenty, Wynn signed his first recording contract with the independent label Intro. His first releases were "I've Waited a Lifetime" and "Strolling," the latter of which caught the attention of Skeets McDonald, an early honky-tonker and mentor. Skeets set up an audition with Ken Nelson of Capitol Records, with positive results.

In 1956, Wynn recorded for Capitol Records. His first hits were "Waltz of the Angels" and "The Keeper of the Key." He used Skeet's band on the session, and Eddie Cochran played guitar. "Waltz of the Angels" was released in July of 1956 and went to Number 14 on the country music charts. This was a rough time for country artists, with Elvis controlling all of the charts and everyone trying to do crossover pop and rock and roll songs. Wynn recorded four more singles with Capitol, but was not thrilled with the idea of adding pop elements to his music.

Wynn's friend, songwriter Harlan Howard, introduced him to Joe Johnson, who headed up a label called Challenge that was owned by Gene Autry. Wynn signed with the label on June 9, 1958. He later teamed up with Jan Howard, the then-wife of Harlan

Howard, and they recorded several albums together. Wynn also recorded for the Jackpot Label, a part of Challenge Records. His first recording was a rockabilly tune called "Come On." He tried to do crossovers with "She Just Tears Me Up" and "Long Black Limousine," but he was only played on country stations, so by 1958, Wynn recorded only country material. In 1959, he cut "Above and Beyond" on the Challenge Label with some success. Buck Owens recorded it later on Capitol Records with Wynn's help.

Wynn was very influential in Buck Owens' career. He liked Buck's work and helped him get a contract with Capitol Records. Ken Nelson had known Buck for some time, but was never interested in giving him a contract. In the late fifties, Wynn pitched a tape of Buck's to Ken, and even though he was not interested, Wynn was persistent. Finally Nelson relented and signed Buck to Capitol Records on August 30, 1957.

Buck's recording style was greatly influenced by Wynn, and even before his first recording, Buck studied Wynn's style. The honky-tonk attitude was there from the start. Buck and Wynn were both style-minded men, and good at arranging works with various hooks. Also, Wynn's steel guitar player, Ralph Mooney, was on Buck's early recordings with that honky-tonk, steel guitar driving sound that was called '60s West Coast Country at that time.

In 1959, Wynn released "Wishful Thinking." His sister Beverly co-wrote the song with him and sang harmony on the record. Ralph Mooney played steel guitar, and Gordon Terry played fiddle. The tune stayed on the charts for twenty-two weeks and peaked at Number 5. I was doing DJ work in Bakersfield at the time, and I remember we played this song repeatedly. In 1960, Wynn recorded a duet with Jan Howard titled "Wrong Company" that went to Number 26 on the country music charts.

In the early sixties, times were good for country music again. The charts, no longer dominated by rock material, were reporting new country hits, and fiddles and steel guitars were back and sounding great. During this time, Wynn was appearing six nights a week at Georges Roundup in Long Beach, California, hosting a show on KFOX and working on a Sunday afternoon television show called "Cal's Corral."

Around this time, 4 Star Music teamed me up with Wynn Stewart's band to do some demos at their studio in Pasadena, California. Wynn's guitar player was a young man named Cecil Bays. He had a sound very much like Hank Garland, one of the great session players in Nashville at the time. Carl Belew was one of the writers there at 4 Star and already had some of his songs recorded, such as "Lonely Street" by Andy Williams and "Am I That Easy to Forget" by Debbie Reynolds. Carl's record on Decca, "Stop the World and Let Me Off," featured his own release of "Am I That Easy to Forget." We began producing demos to present to Patsy Cline and her producer Owen Bradley. She liked Cecil's guitar work, so we hit it off with Patsy and she recorded seven of our songs.

It was during this time that I first met Wynn. Carl Belew was a friend of Wynn's, and one afternoon in 1959,

Carl was using Wynn's band and recording one of my songs called "My Baby's Not Here." Wynn stopped by to say hello to his band and Carl. The session was just starting and the engineer ask Wynn, "Where's your guitar?" Cecil told him to "go get it," which he did, and Wynn played twin guitar on the track. I am very proud of that record. It received a lot of airplay, and because of Wynn's arrangement ideas, it received a lot of notice. It peaked at Number 3 on Cash Box and was recorded by Porter Wagoner on RCA. It was later recorded by Norma Jean on RCA and Rusty Draper on Monument using a brass section.

I got to know Wynn better when I became Buck Owens' bandleader in the fall of 1960. We would often work with Wynn and Ralph Mooney on various shows in Northern California. He was a good showman. When he ended a song, he would raise his right knee up and move it in a twist like movement on the tag. The girls loved it.

Wynn performed at a club in Las Vegas in the early sixties on weeknights, and he hired a young Merle Haggard as a bass player. During this time, Wynn wrote "Sing a Sad Song," intending to record it for his next release. Merle heard him sing it on the show one night and knew it was a song he had to have, so a few days later, he decided to ask Wynn about the song. He said "Wynn, if you had it in your power to make me a star would you do it?" Wynn said, "Sure I would." Merle said, "It is within your power, give me that 'Sing a Sad Song.'" Wynn gave him the song, and Merle first recorded it for Tally Records. If you listen to that recording, you can hear the strong influence of Wynn Stewart.

Wynn's contribution to the birth of the Bakersfield Sound was monumental. He brought the "Town South of Bakersfield" into the picture. He was a huge influence to both Buck Owens and Merle Haggard, and his influence on the Bakersfield Sound lives on.

Afterword: Ralph Mooney's Death

The passing of Ralph Mooney on March 20, 2011 was a sad day for his family and friends who knew and loved him, and a big loss for country music. Ralph was a very creative musician. His co-writing of the song "Crazy Arms" with his friend Chuck Seals changed the sound of country music. It introduced the shuffle and brought back the fiddle and the steel guitar. The new sound paved the way for a lot of new artists in the late fifties. Ralph worked with Wynn Stewart from the time he was a young man onward. Ralph developed a hard-driving, honky-tonk sound that served Wynn so well and influenced Buck Owens. Ralph's work on Buck's early recordings marked the creation of the Bakersfield Sound. Mooney was to the Bakersfield Sound what Chet Atkins was to the Nashville Sound.

I had the privilege of sharing the stage with Ralph Mooney many times in the early days with the Buck Owens show. We did package shows with Wynn Stewart, Bobby Bare, Roger Miller, and Rose and Cal Maddox. What a great time we had. Ralph will be missed, and he will be long remembered for his contribution to the Bakersfield Sound.

THE POLITICIAN—
JIMMY THOMASON

Jimmy Thomason developed his skills as a swing fiddle player when he went to work for W. Lee "Pappy" O'Daniel, the future governor of Texas, in 1936. O'Daniel had been the announcer and partner to The Light Crust Doughboys, Bob Wills' old Texas band. When Wills left, O'Daniel formed W. Lee O'Daniel's Hillbilly Boys. Jimmy was referred to as "Caesar the Fiddle Teaser" on O'Daniel's radio program.

In 1944, Jimmy Thomason became a right-hand man to another soon-to-be governor, Jimmy Davis. Davis was running in Louisiana against Republican governor Earl Long. Davis' song "You Are My Sunshine" had already become a signature song, and he used his Sunshine Band as a campaign tool. With his experience in W. Lee O'Daniel's band, Thomason joined the Sunshine Band playing the fiddle. When Davis won the governor's seat, he appointed Jimmy Thomason Louisiana's Secretary of Defense and Secretary of the Board of Tax Appeals. Now Thomason was a musician, a politician, and an office holder.

Jimmy Davis left office in 1948. He bought a nightclub in Palm Springs and named it The Stables. Thomason and his wife Louise soon joined Davis there, but before they reported to Palm Springs, they visited Bakersfield. Louise's family now lived there, having migrated to Bakersfield in 1941. Jimmy visited some clubs, checking out the music scene, and found Bill Woods at the Clover Club. Jimmy introduced himself and explained his work with Jimmy Davis. Bill invited him to sit in for a couple of numbers, so Jimmy played fiddle and sang for the crowd at the Clover Club. Thomason would later recall their meeting, saying, "No one else wanted to talk to me, acting as if I might take their job."

When Thomason met Davis in Palm Springs, Davis said they needed a piano player. So Thomason called Woods. Woods and Thomason worked together in the Jimmy Davis Band for about a year or so. Davis also headed a national show on CBS from The Stables, and the Thomasons were performers on the show. Jimmy played fiddle and was the bandleader, and his wife Louise was the featured vocalist on each show.

In 1950, after two years in the desert, Davis and his wife returned to Louisiana. Davis and Thomason were good friends for the rest of Davis' life. He died at the age of 101 in 2000. After Davis and his wife left Palm Springs, the Thomasons moved to Bakersfield to be near Louise's family. With the help of Bill Woods, Jimmy landed a job as a radio announcer on Bakersfield's KAFY.

In September of 1953, Jimmy Thomason convinced the folks at KAFY TV, what would later be KBAK TV Channel 29, that a daily country show would sell. They were unsure and thought that Bakersfield was not ready for a country show, but the politician in Thomason prevailed, and they agreed on a two-year contract for "The Jimmy Thomason Show." The band members were Jimmy on fiddle, Louise on vocals, Gene Moles on electric guitar, Cliff Crofford on trumpet and vocals, Ray Heath on drums, and Johnny Barnett on rhythm guitar and vocals. The show was a success. Cousin Herb Henson went on the air a week or so later, but each had their own style. Jimmy's show had the feel of a production with more swing-type music, and Herb's "The Trading Post Show" was more honky-tonk driven because of Herb's piano style.

Thomason, still impressed by Jimmy Davis' success in politics, decided to try to follow in his footsteps. He stepped down from the show after a few months to enter the June primary against Republican incumbent, Senator Jesse R. Dorsey. Louise took over as host for the show to finish out the contract.

Jimmy lost the election, and with the television contract complete, Jimmy and Louise left Bakersfield and returned to Waco, Texas to be near Jimmy's family. He soon started a show there on Waco-TV called "The Home Folks Show." They were there for two years before returning to Bakersfield, this time for a three-year run. Jimmy had an easy style of hosting his television show, and his way of introducing the talent always came across as warm and professional in a way that made them feel good and special to the team. Jimmy went over to KERO-TV for another round of television, this time lasting eight and a half years.

In the early sixties, I had a DJ show on the country radio station KUZZ. Jimmy would often drop by to talk shop and everything else. The man knew everyone. Wade Ray was a singer and fiddle player loaded with talent and showmanship who often played at the Blackboard. He was also a friend of mine, and it was fun to get Jimmy and Wade together and hear them talk.

Jimmy had to give up the show on KERO TV when his health began to fail in 1974, but he was not ready to call it quits just yet. In 1975, he began teaching country music at California State University. I never had the opportunity to stop in for a lecture, but I'm sure it would have been fun. Many of these lectures I had heard before in conversations with Jimmy and Wade Ray.

Jimmy passed away in 1994 at the age of 76. His contribution to the birth of the Sound was his preparation and his professional way of doing his work. His calm stage manner, dress, and attitude all rubbed off on the young entertainers who worked for and with him on his television shows. Many went on to successful careers in country music, and some were huge contributors to the birth of the Sound. Buck Owens, Cliff Crofford, Tommy Collins, Ferlin Husky, Merle Haggard, and Billy Mize were all high on the list. Jimmy also provided work and a forum where these performers could work at their trade and develop their talent.

His dedication to country music helped keep the fan base local, to support the bands and the clubs in Bakersfield. His salesmanship helped keep the business community and radio and television audiences involved. Jimmy and Louise Thomason are still fondly remembered in the San Joaquin Valley.

THE COUNTRY GENTLEMAN—
JOHNNY BARNETT SR.

Johnny Barnett Sr. was born in Minnekah, Oklahoma on April 19, 1918. He was orphaned at age seven and raised by his uncle and older brother. At age eleven, he received his first guitar. By thirteen, he was playing for school dances. At age twenty, he moved to Plainview, Texas where he met and married his first wife.

It was a struggle to make a living there, so they left Texas in 1940 and headed for California where Johnny landed his first job picking apricots in the San Joaquin Valley. During the war years, Johnny worked in Southern California shipyards and continued playing music wherever he could. He knew a lot of songs and liked to sing.

Johnny was able to go to work for Bob Warner at the Lucky Spot club in Bakersfield, and soon took over as leader of a band called The Happy Go Lucky Boys. The other band members were Gene Moles on guitar, Jimmy Wright on drums, Cliff Crofford on vocals, bass and trumpet, and Billy Mize on steel guitar and vocals.

Over the years, many of Bakersfield's great musicians worked at the Lucky Spot, including a new kid who was hired two nights per week to give Barnett some rest. His name was Merle Haggard. Red Simpson and Merle Haggard's song "You Don't Have Very Far to Go" came out of the Lucky Spot.

In 1953, Johnny and part of his band joined the Jimmy Thomason TV Show on KBAK TV, the first daily country show on Bakersfield television. It served as a great advertisement forum and a great way to show the talent Bakersfield had to offer.

Johnny was a working man. After he left the Lucky Spot at 2:00 a.m., he would sleep for a couple of hours, and at 5:00 a.m., he would work a milk route. He kept this pace up until 1963, when he left the music business for a while. He moved to Ridgecrest to work a milk route a year or so, then he moved to the Lone Pine area of the upper desert and later to Bishop, California. He began playing music there two nights a week for twelve years. In the mid-seventies, he returned to Bakersfield. Johnny enjoyed a long and busy life, raising six children.

Johnny's contribution to the birth of the Sound was his twelve years of work at the Lucky Spot and on local television, holding crowds, and giving employment to the young musicians so they could work their craft. Guys like Cliff Crofford, Red Simpson, and Merle Haggard owe at least part of their success to Johnny. The experience those performers gathered while working for him gave them time to learn and develop the knowledge of how to please an audience and how a song must have a dance feel to it. Listening to a Bakersfield writer's song should make a person want to dance. These writers and musicians always found a place for your feet.

Johnny's son, Johnny Barnett Jr. is a fine country drummer whom I've had the pleasure of sharing the stage with. Johnny carries on his father's work and spirit, and the Bakersfield fans and dance crowd fondly remember Johnny Barnett.

Johnny passed away in June of 2007 at the age of eighty-nine and was laid to rest at Hillcrest Memorial park in Bakersfield. His service was attended by many of his fans and fellow musicians. Following the funeral services, a gathering was held at Buck Owens' Crystal Palace to celebrate his life and work with an afternoon of music and tributes to Johnny as Bakersfield said goodbye to a gentle and kind man.

THE MAN OF MANY HATS—
CLIFFIE STONE

Cliffie Stone was born Clifford Gilpin Snyder in Stockton, California on March 1, 1917 to Nina Belle and Clifford H. Snyder, also known as "Herman the Hermit." Cliffie was raised in Burbank, California in the heart of the entertainment world, and with a father in show business, Cliffie began his career with his family. At sixteen, Cliffie worked on Stuart Hamblin's "Lucky Stars" radio show, and later on had his own show. In the beginning, he was known as "Cliffie Stonehead." He would say in later years, "I lost my head and became 'Cliffie Stone.'"

In the forties, Cliffie would do up to twenty-eight shows a week. He performed with a band at the defense plants during World War II, worked as a bass player with the big bands of Anson Weeks and Freddie Slack, and loved working at the Pasadena Playhouse doing comedy sketches for Ken Murray's "Hollywood Blackouts." Cliffie also became a disc jockey, and played a huge role in promoting country and western music in California. He became a fixture at the radio station KXLA in Pasadena with his midday show "Hometown Jamboree," originally known as "Dinner Bell Round

Up." This show led him to the Disc Jockey's Hall of Fame in 1979.

From 1949 to 1960, Cliffie headed one of the first country television shows in the Los Angeles area, also called "Hometown Jamboree," on KTLA Channel 5. A few years earlier, he heard Ernie Ford on a radio station in San Bernardino, liked his personality, and encouraged him to join the radio disc jockeys on KXLA. Ford became a star on Cliffie's television program, began his recording career on Capitol Records, and went on to international stardom. He asked Cliffie to be his manager, and the deal was made on a handshake one day on a hunting trip.

Cliffie hosted many country artists on his "Hometown Jamboree" television show, several of them Bakersfield entertainers like Tommy Collins, Ferlin Husky, Jean Shepherd, Buck Owens, and Cousin Herb Henson. Cousin Herb was a big fan, and was influenced in a big way by Cliffie. Herb called his own midday radio show on KUZZ "The Dinner Bell Jamboree," and he did comedy like Cliffie. Some of the local stars of "Hometown Jamboree" were Ernie Ford, Merle Travis, Molly Bee, Billy Liebert, Jimmy Bryant, Speedy West, "Herman the Hermit," Gene O'Quinn, and Billy Strange. Also featured were sisters Jeanie and Janie Black, Joanie O'Brian, Dallas Frazier, Billy Armstrong, Ferlin Husky, Tommy Sands, Barbara Mandrell, Les "Carrot Top" Anderson, Tex Williams, Eddie Dean, and Freddie Hart, his long-time friend and band mate Wesley Tuttle, and his wife Marilyn.

Liberace made the show from time to time, and even Elvis appeared once. Many of the country and western stars of the day would also appear on the "Jamboree," such as Eddie Arnold, Lefty Frizzell, Johnny Cash, and Jim Reeves, to name a few.

In the forties, Cliffie joined Capitol Records as a recording artist and head of the Country and Western Department. He began signing artists who would become major stars, such as Merle Travis, Johnny Bond, Tex Ritter, Tommy Collins, Faron Young, and Tennessee Ernie Ford.

Cliffie also added the publishing company Central Songs to his enterprising world. Some of the songs Cliffie was affiliated with as a publisher of Central Songs that would be a part of the Bakersfield Sound catalog were "Under Your Spell Again," recorded by Buck Owens and written by Buck and Dusty Rhodes; "Under the Influence of Love," also recorded by Buck and written by Harlan Howard and Buck; "Foolin' Around," recorded by Buck Owens and Harlan Howard; and "Together Again," written and recorded by Buck Owens.

Stone first became a major name and influence in 1946 when three songs he co-wrote reached Top Five on the country and western charts—"No Vacancy" with Merle Travis, "New Steel Guitar Rag" with Bill Boyd and the Cowboy Ramblers, and three different recordings of "Divorce Me C.O.D." by Johnny Bond, the King Sisters, and Merle Travis. He also had his own recordings with his band doing songs like "Silver Stars," "Purple Sage," "Peepin' Through the Keyhole,"

"When My Blue Moon Turns to Gold Again," and "Little Pink Mack."

Cliffie was a good friend and supporter of the artists from Bakersfield, and was very aware of the talent and the country scene throughout the San Joaquin Valley. He worked closely with Ken Nelson in promoting the artists from Bakersfield, such as Ferlin Husky, Jean Shepard, Tommy Collins, Buck Owens, Merle Haggard, and Red Simpson. Cliffie also provided songs and/or publishing when needed.

Cliffie wore many hats. It is said that he produced more than 14,000 radio and television shows, including Tennessee Ernie's "The Ernie Ford Show" on NBC. He was also a wonderful bass player, comedian, singer, songwriter, manager, publisher, recording artist, bandleader, disc jockey, business executive, author, and friend.

Cliffie Stone received many awards and honors over the years. He was inducted into the Country Music Hall of Fame in 1979, and in 1989 the California Country Music Hall of Fame. He also received a star on Sunset and Vine on the Hollywood Walk of Fame. In the late eighties, I had the honor of introducing him when he was awarded The Pioneer Award by the California Country Music Association. He also served as vice president of the Country Music Association, and the president and a director of the Academy of Country Music.

Cliffie was going to write the forward for this book, but passed away before we reached that point. Cliffie Stone died from a heart attack at the age of eighty on

January 17, 1998 in his Canyon Country home. He is survived by his wife Joan, and his four children, Curtis, Linda, Steven, and Jonathan.

Stone's contribution to the birth of the Bakersfield Sound is far-reaching and stretches all the way back to the beginning. His support was strong and faithful, not only to the recording artists, but to the musicians as well. He was always happy when someone reached a level of success, and he wanted to share it with them. He considered himself part of the team with the Bakersfield artists. Those who played a part in the birth of the Bakersfield Sound will long remember Cliffie Stone.

THE BOSS—KEN NELSON

Ken Nelson was born on January 19, 1911 in Caledonia, Minnesota. He began his career in Chicago at radio station WJJD doing clerical work, announcing, and whatever other odd jobs needed doing. He was interested in both pop and classical music, and became announcer for the broadcast by the Chicago Symphony Orchestra. He was also put in charge of the "Suppertime Frolic Hillbilly Show," the beginning of a lot of frolic shows around the country. Ken's job was to audition and find talent, and he began to travel all around the Southwest and Midwest, and learning a great deal about the popularity of country music in the process.

In the '40s, Ken went to Hollywood to take over the transcription department of Capitol Records. In 1951, his old friend from Chicago, Lee Gillette, transferred from Chief of Country A & R to A & R of the pop department. Nelson became head of the country department. One of Ken's first sessions was with Hank Thompson, who was already a popular artist. His recording produced by Nelson, a tune by the name of "The Wild Side of Life," was a huge Number 1 success. This not only boosted Thompson's career, it also lifted Capitol Records to prominence in country music.

Nelson continued to travel and go to events, concerts, nightclubs, and even to bus stations listening to juke boxes to learn what the country was listening to. He worked closely with Cliffie Stone, who was now with Capitol. Lee Gillette and the two of them founded Central Songs, a publishing company that grew fast and became one of the largest in the industry. Ken and Cliffie signed such artists to the label as Ferlin Husky, Jean Shepard, Tommy Collins, Wynn Stewart, Faron Young, Wanda Jackson, Jerry Reed, Rose Maddox, Red Simpson, Glen Campbell, Buck Owens, and Merle Haggard, who would become top acts of the 1960s.

In college, Ken Nelson was an entertainer himself, singing and playing banjo in his easy style. In the mid-fifties, he learned that Rockabilly music moved people in a very special way. The success of Elvis Presley was a big lesson. Ken joined the rock and roll crowd early and signed Gene Vincent. This led him to signing artists who had their own style and their own band, folks like Wynn Stewart, Hank Thompson, Jerry Reed, Glenn Campbell, Buck Owens, and Merle Haggard. He would have his engineer set up the session, make suggestions, share ideas, then he would let the artists go to work. He dressed in a casual manner, sweater vests and cardigans, which set everyone at ease. Close to two hundred artists worked under Nelson's direction, producing thousands of songs and arrangements and more than 100 Number 1 hits.

Ken played such an important role in the birth of the Bakersfield Sound. When he met with Bill Woods, Fuzzy Owen, Lewis Talley, and Ferlin Huskey regarding the recording of "Dear John Letter," Ken turned it down. He said it was a war song, and there was no war, but he eventually relented when he saw the passion of this group of determined men. One of Nelson's gifts was his ability to see beyond the audition of the artist and see the future. Thanks to that foresight, these men were rewarded with the first number one hit song out of Bakersfield.

"Dear John Letter" put Bakersfield on the map and introduced Jean Shepard and Ferlin Huskey to a national audience. This song reflects Ken Nelson's fondness for a hard-driving, honky-tonk sound, and marks the cornerstone for the birth of the Bakersfield Sound.

Without Ken Nelson's contribution, the Sound may not have reached the height of popularity and recognition it received during the sixties. His work influenced many rock stars. Even the Beatles wanted to have each new Buck Owens recording. Nelson was a leader in forming the Country Music Association (CMA). He retired in 1976, and was elected to the Country Music Hall of Fame in 2001.

Ken Nelson passed away on January 6, 2008 at his home in Somis, California just a few days short of his ninety-seventh birthday. His name and his work will long be remembered. His memory is honored at Buck Owens' Crystal Palace, and his influence lives on in the hearts of fans and many musicians who had the opportunity of working with him and witnessing his contribution to the birth of the Bakersfield Sound.

THE PARTNER—DON RICH

The guitar that added the most to the Bakersfield Sound was the same one that gave Buck Owens' recordings their raw, driving sound. The man who played it was Don Rich.

Don learned his now-famous "Rich licks" from Buck himself. This guitar sound, combined with Buck's ability to pick up the feel of a song, inspired a lot of guitar players and singers, including The Beatles, who had a standing order at Capitol for a copy of every new Buck Owens release.

One of the hardest and most meaningful interviews I did for this book was when I flew to Las Vegas and talked with Don Rich's wife Marlene, who had been married to Don at the time of his unfortunate death.

Don and Marlene were both born in Washington, he from Olympia and she from Mount Rainer. Her parents were Mary and Royal Shindles. When Marlene was very young, her mother became ill, and Marlene's grandparents took her and her brother in. Don and Marlene met as students at Centralia Junior College, and fell deeply in love. However, Don's parents were protective of him, and did not approve of the romance.

Don was adopted at birth and never knew his natural parents. Marlene says she understood his natural father was a soldier at Fort Lewis, but she and Don had no knowledge of his mother. William "Bill" Ulrich and his wife Anna adopted Don, and named him Donald Ulrich.

Don began playing music as a teenager. He signed a Capitol Record contract when he entered college, and there became "Don Rich." During his first year of college, he worked dates throughout Washington State, and taught guitar lessons.

At one show, he met an up-and-coming country entertainer named Buck Owens, who was working in Washington state at the time. This encounter would forever change the lives of both men. Don began working exclusively with Buck at Britannia Tavern in Washington, and they also did radio and television together. In the late fifties, they worked at a place called Breezeman Park.

Don's parents liked Buck and his wife, Phyllis. Buck moved back to Bakersfield, and six months later, Don went down on Christmas break to see him. Don decided to join Buck there, a decision his parents quickly approved of, thinking it would end his relationship with Marlene. They would soon learn the truth about Don and Marlene's love for each other.

This was when I first met 19-year-old Don Rich, while working for Buck Owens in 1960. Don and I became close friends. We would travel to various show dates together, and I was like a big brother to him. I would help him sound out various problems, such as quitting college to work full-time in music with Buck. When we would work the Fresno barn, one of our favorite restaurants after work was a place in Kingsburg, California. Don and I would order the same things, either a hot beef sandwich with lots of brown gravy, or hot chili with 100 crackers. We both loved chili and crackers, and we would sit there talking for the longest time. He was young and eager, and he worked endlessly on his guitar and fiddle. Marlene told me, "He played guitar all the time and I loved it, but when he practiced the fiddle, it was something else…"

Don did well in his time living with Buck and Phyllis. Buck could work with him day and night, and Don was the perfect one to interpret Buck's music. The two were like twins, always knowing the others every thought. Though they were never billed as a duet, they were better than that.

While we were traveling down some highway, Don would talk of Marlene, how he missed her, how everything reminded him of her. He would speak of his parents with deep respect and concern. They were well into middle age when they adopted him, and he was concerned for them and knew how much they missed him. He was grateful for all they had done for him, yet troubled over how everything would work out.

Don's parents came down to Bakersfield shortly after Don came to town to check things out. They went to some shows with us and would ride with me, asking questions after their son, wanting to know if he was happy and so on. They were wonderful people.

Buck made personal appearances and worked the radio stations promoting his album. He would take Don to Washington as often as he could. On one of these trips, Marlene traveled with them up to a show up near the Washington border of Canada. A young Loretta Lynn was on the show. She lived nearby with her family and her husband "Moonie." She was just getting started, and invited Buck, Don, and Marlene to dinner. Marlene says, "It was something else. She showed us how she sewed her own stage clothes... We were impressed."

Marlene was helping her grandfather, an accountant who had gone blind, do income taxes in Washington. She did the paperwork while he computed the taxes in his head. Don was in California. We talked about love and marriage, and I remember telling him that true love was hard to find. I had met Marlene by then, and had seen them together. I felt it was the right thing, and that she would understand and support his career. After four months of being apart, Don went to Washington, picked up Marlene and they eloped in Las Vegas, one week after April 15th.

Don loved people. He could smile a natural, winning smile, even when burdened. Buck expected total dedication to him and the band from the people he worked with, and together he and Don could make it seem easy. No matter how tired we were, or how bad the weather, or what personal problems we each had, with Buck and Don, as soon as the first note was sounded, the band and the crowd were a happy group.

After the wedding, with that dilemma behind him, Don became very serious and even more dedicated to his career. Each month was busier than the month before, with travel, recording, television, and personal appearances. Their music became more and more in demand as the Bakersfield Sound was being tuned, polished, and recognized worldwide.

Don and Marlene's family changed on January 11, 1963 with the birth of their first son, Vance. Don was on the road doing a television show in Oklahoma City, and could not make it back in time for Vance's birth. Marlene was staying with Phyllis, and Buck's parents were helping out. They even practiced driving to the hospital beforehand, to be prepared. They were ready when she and baby were, and of course, Phyllis was with her. When Don and Buck showed up, Phyllis ran out to the car, and instead of kissing Buck, she ran up and kissed Don. "Well, he was a new father, of course," laughs Marlene. The next morning Don was with Marlene and Vance. He kept touching his face, and suddenly realized that in all the excitement, he'd shaved his face without lather!

Their next son, Vic, was due to be born on October 19, 1964, and again Don was on the road, this time in Green Bay, Wisconsin. The birth was going to be late, so they set a date to induce labor during the break in shows. George Jones was on the show, and he chartered a plane to fly Don into Chicago so Don could make a connection into Los Angeles to be there for Vic's birth. Marlene said she thought "maybe it would be good for him to watch the birth and maybe they wouldn't have any more children. Instead, he kept saying how great it was, and if he was a woman, he would have fifteen of them."

I recall meeting Don for lunch when Marlene was pregnant with Vance. He was so excited about being a father soon, and had all these plans for a big family. After lunch, he showed me the house. We walked into the living room, then into the kitchen. As we walked into the bedroom, still talking about the coming birth, Don said, "This is the workroom."

The next several years after the birth of his sons, time flew by. Don was very busy most of the year, doing world-wide tours, television recordings, and appearing on "Hee Haw." Buck Owens had become one of country music's biggest names, known as the Ambassador of Bakersfield, and had given a definition to the Bakersfield Sound. Don Rich was a big part of that, and his contribution lives on today in much of the guitar sounds you hear on country radio and even in rock music. The drive, the energy, and the spirit live on.

I did not know then, but in the early sixties, when Don was first with the band, guitar players from all over the world would attend the shows and watch Don and Buck and pick up guitar licks. Many of them went on to become rock and roll musicians. Their influence continued to grow in later years. I left the band in the early sixties, but continued to follow their growing popularity and see them on occasion.

Marlene said Don would spend every moment possible with his sons, as if trying to make up for his time away. He would take them fishing, an activity the whole family, including Marlene, loved. He would take them hunting, teaching them about gun safety and how to shoot. Don would spend time talking to his sons, and, knowing him, I'm sure a lot of those talks were about life and feelings. Don was a very sensitive man, and could sense the pain in others. He could read people well, and everyone was his friend. He always had a smile for people. He was close to his family, to his sons, and his family brought feelings he'd only ever dreamed about or talked about in some car traveling down a lonesome highway.

When I heard of Don's death on the radio, I simply could not believe it. There must have been a mistake, and I stayed tuned in for an update. This gentle person was too good, too strong, too smart to go this way. But it was true. As a friend, I said a prayer for Marlene and the boys. I also prayed for Buck, and wondered how he could possibly go on. They were brothers, best friends, and artists who needed each other to draw out the great talent each had inside them.

Don was killed in a motorcycle accident on July 16, 1974, just outside of Morro Bay, California. He was on his way to see Marlene and his sons who were waiting for him in Cambria, California where they were visiting some friends, Jack and Dianne Emmill. Marlene told me about the fateful day.

"Originally we were all going to go over to the coast together and go deep sea fishing. Buck had called a recording session, but Don thought it would be cancelled. It turned out they decided to record, so Don told me to go on over and he would come over afterward. He would drive the sports car when he was through, but the car was making a funny noise, so he decided to ride the motorcycle over.

"The drive from Bakersfield to Cambria is 120 miles. Don assured me he would be real careful. He went by Doyle Holley's house and picked up a gun in case someone tried to run him off the road or something like that. He had his helmet and he told me not to worry, he'd take his time, and if he got tired, he would pull over and sleep. He was carrying a sleeping bag with him just in case. This was all before I left Bakersfield for the fishing trip and when he got off this is what he was going to do.

"So the boys and I went over with our friends and their son. The motel we were staying at had a golf course. After we arrived, the kids and I, along with Jack and Dianne went out to play golf. Later when we went back to the room, there was a message Don was on his way and would be there around 7 or 8 o'clock.

"I waited and waited. At around midnight, he had not showed up, so I put a note on one of the cars telling him what the room number was, and during the time when I was out waiting and watching for him, I did hear sirens, so it could have been the accident! Still he didn't show up and I was a little upset and worried and thought, well he must have gotten tired or something; I couldn't figure out what had happened. But before I left he said if he didn't show up at the hotel to go ahead and go by the San Simeon Pier because that is where we were going to take the boat out, and if he didn't go to the hotel he would go on to the pier.

"So we went there and no Don. We went by all the motels in San Simeon and Cambria. Finally Jack said, 'I'm going to call Marvin Mason,' one of our friends in Bakersfield. So Jack called Marvin and he did not know what had happened, but the police had been by his house looking for me. But what really happened was Marvin told Jack that Don was killed, but Jack did not tell me. He was giving Marvin time to notify the Police Department on the coast of my location. Then later Jack told me the story, and said we will have to go to San Luis Obispo Sheriff's Office so you can identify Don's personal effects. We left. I still had not told the boys. The police met us and escorted us through town. Gee, I said, this is the first time I can remember going through town at sixty miles an hour like this. The police were pushing us through town, past the scene of the accident. I finally told the boys on the way to the Sheriff's Office.

"The next few days were just a blur, a total nightmare. The loss was so hard to accept. The accident occurred just outside of Morro Bay near the last stoplight toward Cayucas. We thought there might have been something, but the police saw him go through the intersection traveling the speed limit. I think maybe an animal might have run in front of the bike, and he veered to avoid hitting it. What actually killed him was the impact of hitting the handlebars. It killed him almost instantly. I guess he controlled the bike pretty well until he ran into a cement girder and he hit his head. His helmet had a crack in it. I didn't go by and see the bike. I didn't want to."

Don was buried at Greenlawn Cemetery in Bakersfield. His funeral was attended by many friends and fans. Letters and wires by the hundreds kept coming in. Country music had lost a great talent, a gentle giant.

In his short career, he and Marlene had done well financially and had acquired several properties. Marlene stayed in Bakersfield two years after Don's death. She remarried in 1976 to Larry Dunivent, a friend of Don's whom she had known for a long time. Larry was in the real estate business and handled their properties. When Vance was fifteen years old, Marlene was pregnant with their son, David. Two years later, she gave birth to Deena, a beautiful, happy girl. At the time of our interview, she was thirteen, "almost fourteen" she was quick to add, and full of life like her mother. Vance and Vic now live in the Los Angeles area and work in the insurance industry. Marlene has one grandson and two granddaughters.

Don would be proud knowing his roots are deep and growing. His music, along with his musical influence, will remain with us forever in our memory. His "Rich licks" can still be heard in many of the records recorded by today's session players. His contribution to the Bakersfield Sound was so large and so deep, words cannot be found to describe it.

THE TELEMASTER—
ROY NICHOLS

Roy Ernest Nichols was born on October 21, 1932 in Chandler, Arizona. He had three brothers, Gene, Larry, and Jimmy, and three sisters, Loretta, Donna, and Wanda. Roy was raised in Fresno, California, and was influenced by the musicians Bob Wills left behind there.

Roy left Fresno and went to Texas at age fifteen. Two weeks before his sixteenth birthday, he went to work playing guitar with the hottest hillbilly road band in the country: The Maddox Brothers and Rose. I went to see them in 1949 in Tulare, California, and was blown away by Roy's aggressive style of play. Billed as "Little Roy Nichols," he helped make the Maddox Brothers and Rose the hottest show band in the country, and recorded over 100 songs with the band. He had to give up school to do this, as the Maddox family was booked seven nights a week year-round. Roy stayed with them for two years, then slowed down some and went to work in Hanford, California with "Smiley" Maxedon.

After a year with Smiley, Roy joined the popular Lefty Frizell show. Lefty became a national legend and a hero to the Bakersfield crowds with songs like

"If You've Got the Money, I've Got the Time" and "Always Late." Lefty became a major influence on a young Merle Haggard, and had a deep impact on the birth of the Bakersfield Sound in general. While with Lefty, Roy often appeared at the Rainbow Gardens in Bakersfield and became acquainted with several of the local musicians.

Some time later, Roy became a member of Cousin Herb Henson's Trading Post Gang on KERO TV five days a week and made special appearances with the Trading Post band. Cliff Crofford said, "The quality of music increased several degrees when Roy came to town." Roy's talents added a big boost to the show's popularity, and his influence on other musicians was immeasurable.

In the late fifties, Roy, Lewis Talley, and Fuzzy Owen worked the upper desert around Ridgecrest, California on Friday and Saturday nights for several years.

In the early sixties, Roy moved to the Long Beach area and began working with Billy Mize and Cliff Crofford at the Foothill Club in Long Beach. Roy and Cliff took a leave of absence from the band in '61 to tour with Johnny Cash. Roy went on to serve a second tour with Cash, but Crofford chose to return to the Foothill Club. It was during that second tour that Cash wrote the song "Tennessee Flat Top Box," a song that carried Roy's influence. When the song was recorded, Roy played on the record.

After the second Johnny Cash tour, Roy returned to the Foothill Club and worked a few months before accepting a job in Las Vegas with Wynn Stewart and Ralph Mooney. He enjoyed working with them.

Roy played a role in Wynn's hiring of Merle Haggard in the early sixties. Merle and his good friend, Dean Holloway, went to Las Vegas on a visit and dropped in at the Nashville Nevada Club to see Wynn Stewart, but Wynn was on break when they arrived. Roy knew Merle some, and when he saw Merle come into the club, Roy handed him his guitar and said, "Play this thing awhile so I can take a break." Merle was somewhat reluctant, but was singing by the time Wynn returned. Wynn stood in the middle of the floor, and when Merle was finished, Wynn bought him a drink and offered him a job as bass player. Merle accepted. He worked in Vegas with Roy and Wynn's band for a while before he returned to Bakersfield to begin his recording career with Lewis Talley and Fuzzy Owen, and then on to Capitol Records.

In August of 1965, Haggard formed his band, The Strangers, and Roy was the first band member he hired. Roy's guitar playing was the style needed for the hard-driving, rockabilly, honky-tonk attitude that was emerging in country music, later called the Bakersfield Sound.

In 1965, Roy was still in Las Vegas and making good money there with Wynn, but he was anxious to join Merle. Merle wrote later that when he asked Roy to join, he said, "I can't pay you what Wynn is paying you, but I think I can make it now, and you can play for me the rest of my life." Roy said he would give his notice. Roy stayed with Merle's band until March

1987, when he retired and settled in Bakersfield with his wife Quita. He continued to play some local shows and did some radio with Bill Woods and Rose and Fred Maddox.

Roy became one of the most imitated guitar players in country music. He could play it all, from rockabilly to jazz and country. He was also a writer with 19 published songs. One song, "Street Singer," was nominated for a Grammy Award in 1970. Even today, his work is remembered and followed. Between the time Roy joined Merle in 1965 to the time Roy left in 1987, the band recorded 38 songs that reached Number 1 in Billboard, and another 33 that reached the Top 10. Roy was inducted into the Western Swing Society Hall of Fame in 1987.

In 1996, Roy suffered a stroke that put him in a wheelchair, and he lost the use of his left hand. He told Cliff Crofford later, "I can only play guitar in my head."

On July 3rd, 2001, at 68 years old, Roy suffered a fatal heart attack, and was buried at Greenlawn Cemetery. He is survived by his wife Chiquita Nichols; daughters Sandy Martin and Diane Nichols Farrow; son Michael Nichols; stepdaughter Jackie Christenson; brothers Gene, Larry "Bo," and Jimmy Nichols; sisters Loretta Gutierrez, Donna Ytteralde and Wanda Benson; grandchildren Kim, Tiffany, Donald, Stephanie, Kristina, Nicole, Jessica, Kady and Whitney; and four great grandchildren.

Roy Nichols was a huge influence on music and one of the major contributors to the birth of the Sound. His many Number 1 recordings with Haggard and others will stand for years to come as a showcase for his musicianship and talent as an artist. Fans will forever remember the thrill and enjoyment of listening to him and seeing him work. His influence lives on. It is interesting to see and hear the work of a very young Benny Haggard, Merle's son, and enjoy his interpretation of the Roy Nichols licks.

SHOTGUN DANIELS— LARRY DANIELS

Bakersfield music was lucky to have Larry Daniels in the early sixties. His career began in high school when one of his teachers raised his interest in radio. He asked a local station, KGEN in Tulare, California, if he could do odd jobs at the studio in exchange for an education in radio.

A short time later Larry Daniels was on the air. In the late fifties, the station was sold and the new ownership changed the format from pop to country. I began listening to the station, and in 1959 I dropped by the station and met Larry. I took him a single of Patsy Cline's "Let the Teardrops Fall" and asked if he would perhaps play it. Although young at the time, Larry was very sincere and professional, and we became friends.

In the early '60s, I was working for the newly formed country radio station KUZZ, and I put Larry's name forward as a disc jockey for the station. An interview was set up, and he found a home at KUZZ under the moniker "Shotgun Daniels." Not long later, another award winning disc jockey, Larry "Boothill" Scott, joined KUZZ. Frank "Tombstone" Morgan joined the station sometime after that as well. Well versed in country music, these men were the perfect trio to support the birth of the Bakersfield Sound on radio. They did interviews with many of the stars booked in town by Herb Henson and Bill Woods.

Around this time, Daniels also formed a band called The Buckshots. He hired a bass player named Doyle Holly, a steel player named Larry Petree, who was with me and The Valley Rhythm Boys for five or six years, a drummer named Jimmy Phillips, and a piano player named Bill Vibe. Buck Owens would book other country stars for shows in the area, and Larry's band would front them.

Larry was instrumental in helping Buck Owens build his broadcasting business. In 1965, Buck bought KUZZ, and Larry and Buck's relationship was sealed. In 1971, after 10 years of hard work in Bakersfield, Daniels became program director for Buck's country stations in Phoenix, KTUF AM and KNIX FM. They worked together for close to 30 years, and their award winning stations were successful. The stations were sold in 1999 to Clear Channel.

Larry's contribution to the birth of the Bakersfield Sound covers a lot of ground. He helped with building a strong broadcast base, and stayed with the country format through the years. He was rewarded and recognized as a radio great on February 27, 1997 when he was enshrined in the Radio Hall of Fame in Nashville, Tennessee, capping a 50-year career in broadcasting.

Larry is now a self-employed radio consultant. His company is called "Country Radio Resources" and is located in Phoenix. His first client was KUZZ. He makes his home in Tempe, Arizona with his lovely wife Marilyn, whom he met and married in my hometown of Delano, California. He was chosen to deliver the eulogy at Buck Owens' funeral on March 25, 2006. It had to be quite an experience for Larry after some 30 years of working with and for Buck.

Larry still visits Bakersfield from time to time as part of the Bakersfield Country Music Museum Show, and he performs on some of the shows. He is a KUZZ legend and a big contributor to the birth of the Bakersfield Sound.

THE VALLEY RHYTHM BOYS—
LAWTON JILES

My father, Jess Jiles, and my mother, Tressie, were married in Long, Oklahoma in February of 1929. My father was nineteen and my mother was twenty. Soon after they were married, they left for Caruthers, California, a farming community outside of Fresno where my mother's sister, Vella, lived with her husband, Arthur Woodward. Not long after the move, my mother discovered she was pregnant with me, her first child.

My mother's uncle, Tom Howell, was a big landowner in Eastern Oklahoma, and when the stock market crashed, his tenants on the farmland began leaving. He asked if my father would return to Oklahoma to help him settle these affairs. They were young and uneasy with her first pregnancy, so my mother and father decided to return to Oklahoma. I was born in December. My parents worked with Uncle Tom for two years before returning to the farm in California. My father worked the equipment there, and we lived on the property in a house furnished by the company.

I remember as a three- or four-year-old listening to the music in that house. My dad played guitar and sang folk songs, my mom played Dobro and slide guitar, and my cousin Ralph Woodward, who was around sixteen at the time, played guitar. The crew that was in charge of taking care of the landscape of the three houses and office area would often stop on our front porch. My mother would bring my dad's guitar out, and they would all play some Mexican music. It was so exciting for me, and I remember it to this day.

My cousin Ralph knew the Lewis boys, Ford and Glen, and they were also into music. Ford went on to a long career in the forties with songs like "You're My Angel, Judy." They would all show up at our place for a music get-together, and as a child, my brother Johnnie, who was born in 1932, and I would sit in the corner and listen to those songs and the stories they would tell.

These boys were also friends with the singer-songwriter Woody Guthrie and his cousin Jack, who were in and around Fresno during the Depression. The Louis boys had a radio show in Fresno for a while, and that is where my brother Johnny and I got our interest in music.

In the early forties, we moved to Delano, California, where we learned to play guitar. My mother had the most patience with us, and our father would encourage us and help teach us the songs. I was working on the fiddle and the steel guitar, and my brother was learning to play lead guitar.

As teenagers in the mid-forties, we would play at parties and small events. The late forties were exciting years because Hank Williams, Hank Thompson, Earnest Tubb, T. Texas Tyler, Eddy Arnold, Bob Wills, Tommy Duncan and others were writing and doing a new style of country music. We were into this in a serious way.

In high school we started playing more and more events. In August 1948, one of our friends, Dick Chaney, told us his father wanted to see us. He owned a small café in Richgrove, California. It was near the Tulare and Kern County line, a quarter-mile east of the Kern County line. Mr. Chaney told us that if we could get a band together, he would set us up at his Blue Moon Café. We had a Tommy Duncan-style lead singer by the name of "Jewel" Red White, but we did not have a drummer. Dick was interested, but did not have a drum set. We heard about a drum set for sale in Ducor, California, and went over to have a look. We found a nice set of Pearl drums, and Dick decided he would like to try them. He bought them, and we went home and did our woodshed thing. We worked on our music for about ten days. At the time, Dick and Johnny were not quite sixteen, Red was twenty-one, and I was almost eighteen.

The band did not have a smooth start. We had trouble starting together, staying together, and stopping together. Despite all that, sometime around August we began playing at the Blue Moon Café on a Friday night. The place was a huge success, but not because of the band. Because of its location out in the country, there was no Sheriff's Department, no police, and one constable for the western end of the county who would hardly ever come around. It was a rowdy crowd that would gather on Friday and Saturday nights to drink, dance, fight, or make love in the parking lot.

There were always as many people outside as there were inside. Fights were organized a week in advance, saying "I will see you at the Blue Moon next Friday night." It was like the Western movies, and the winner would have to be challenged by someone the next weekend, women the same as men. Sometimes there were several fights on both nights. The difference was that in those days after the fight, sometimes they would shake hands and buy each other a beer and there were no guns involved. The club had firm instructions for us that when a fight broke out, just keep the music going, do not stop for another song, just keep the music playing.

On one Saturday night, the place emptied fast. Everyone was out, the bartenders, the waitresses, the bouncer, all of them just up and gone. Red, the bandleader, stopped and said, "Oh, this one must be something big. Let's go see." We got to the back door, and we could see a hundred people or so calling to us to run, to get out of there. We began to move out, but not fast enough, so they kept on yelling to run, run, and so we did. A young man had brought his girl to the club, and a dispute developed when she danced with someone else. He planted a stick of dynamite on top of the band stand area built on the side of the café. It so happened the fuse came out of the dynamite, or we would have been gone. Some big old boy who looked like Paul Bunyan had the young man, and was punching him up and down the alley. We were so eager to play music, we even went back in, but not before we had a new understanding about informing the band of certain dangers. Our parents never heard of these events, and we were careful to hide them, or we would have been out of The Blue Moon Café.

By 1950, we had changed the style of the band to have more swing influence. We listened to a lot of Bakersfield radio shows, like Bob Wills' 15-minute recorded program and Billy Mize's 15-minute show on KAFY, and Bill Woods had a radio show that kept us up to date on what was new in country music. We would learn new songs and pick up ideas from radio. We were shortly joined by Dean Trammel, an excellent fiddle player with a professional background. We were playing more dance halls, theaters and special events now, but the Korean War was looming, and I was the right age.

On January 8, 1951, I found myself playing in a new band—the U.S. Air Force. My brother Johnny took over the band back home and kept it going. I settled into military life and met some other musicians in the military, and we would play together when we could.

I also visited bands and clubs off base and worked on writing some songs. My dad was a writer who would write story songs about anything that caught his attention. His ability to tell a story influenced me to become a writer. Some other songwriters who influenced me were Hank Williams, Cindy Walker, Fred Rose, and Tommy Duncan. I was inspired by the singing talent of Hank Williams, Eddy Arnold, Jimmy Rogers, and Tommy Duncan.

I was discharged in 1953 and returned to Delano, California where I worked several jobs while getting the band going again. Johnny had kept the band playing in clubs, but I wanted to move into dance halls in the San Joaquin Valley. The music scene had changed. Bakersfield had a new group of musicians, and radio was everywhere. Thad Buckley, so dubbed "The Catalina Cowboy" by Bill Woods, was doing great work as a DJ on KCHJ radio station. Jimmy Thomason would soon be on television, with Cousin Herb and "The Trading Post Show" not far behind. The Korean War was ending, and life was great.

The Valley Rhythm Boys started slowly. Larry Petree, a steel guitar player, came on board, followed by Del Baker, a fiddle player who also played piano. We were now a swing band, playing local dance halls with Dean Trammel on fiddle. We used Del for twin fiddle tunes. My brother Johnny played lead and helped on vocals, and I was now fronting the band on rhythm and vocals. The band members changed some through the years. In 1954, I made my first television appearance on the Cousin Herb Show with Bill Woods, Tommy Collins, and Billy Mize. I recall being very nervous.

I began working some with Bill Woods, doing some demo work, and a little later, recorded my first record on Bakersfield Records. Woods was producing and playing bass, Buck Owens was on guitar, Johnny Cuviello was on drums, and I played rhythm. The A side was "Million Miles Between Us," and the B side was "Crazy Over You." At Christmas time, we did one more record, a song called "Santa Claus Forgot Me" with Tootsie Lee and the same musicians. These were all recorded at Ed Smizer's studio out on Belle Terrace.

Later, I recorded for the King label. My biggest success was with a song we co-wrote with Carl Belew called "You're Not That Easy to Forget." The flipside was "That's What I Get for Lovin' You," recorded with the Wynn Stewart band.

As time went along, music changed. The late fifties were tough years. Record companies were all looking for another Elvis. It was a great time for artists who were able to move into rock, but country took a hard hit, and the fiddle and steel guitar were out. At one point, Elvis had most of the Top 10 country positions on Billboard.

The Valley Rhythm Boys were no exception to the changing musical climate. We had to adapt and play a lot of rock and roll and rhythm and blues tunes. The club with the most success during this time of transition was probably the Blackboard Café in Bakersfield with Bill Woods and his band of Buck Owens, Don Markham on sax, Johnny Cuviello on drums, and later Henry Sharp.

The band and I took a job at the Cellar Club in Delano. During this time, we had a young crowd, so we did a mix of country and rock, and we still worked the dance hall circuit on weekends. We would also work with a local radio KCHJ personality named Bob Scott. We would do remote broadcasts on weekends throughout the area working on the back of a flatbed truck. We'd sometimes hit four or five different locations on a Saturday, all on Radio KCHJ in Delano, and we featured different guests, sideshow stunts, animals, and so on.

We began a nightly radio show on KCHJ, broadcast time nine p.m. We were concerned about the time slot, but it served us well. The station was a 10,000-watt clear channel, and it covered the San Joaquin. We could advertise a show in Fresno, a show on the on the coast, or even a show in the upper desert, all of the regions we worked in.

The Valley Rhythm Boys didn't do too badly. We never recorded a record, but Dean Trammel, the fiddle player for the Valley Rhythm Boys for close to fifteen years, was inducted into America's Old Time Fiddlers Hall of Fame in the early '90s. Del Baker, who doubled on fiddle and piano, was also inducted into the Fiddlers Hall of Fame in 2000. Dean Trammel had nominated him for the year 2000 before Dean passed away in 1999. They had played twin fiddle together for forty years, and I was very proud and happy for them. Lavonia Morrison, who sang with us for a while, won several awards, including BMI gold and platinum for her song "Act Naturally." Larry Petree, the steel player, has become much acclaimed, played on countless records, and was a founding member of the Bakersfield Country Music Museum. He still works on many shows in the Bakersfield area. My brother Johnny was such a big help to me. He also played bass guitar on Cousin Herb's show.

In 1959, Bob Scott, a radio man I had worked with in Delano, came to me saying he heard about a station in Bakersfield that was playing rhythm and blues. The station was not doing well, and Bob explained how he would like to start an all-country station. We talked about it and decided Bob would go to Los Angeles the next day and talk to Mr. Arnoff, the owner. He made a management purchase deal and came back to Bakersfield just before nightfall. It was decided we would go on the air the next morning with country music. We worked most of the night trying to find country records, and I cornered Bill Woods, who would later become a DJ, and got all the records I could from him to add together with mine. I called Billy Garner, a lead guitar player with the Valley Rhythm Boys, and talked him into going on the air at 6:00 a.m. the next day. It was a 500-watt clear channel, a daytime station sun up to sun down, 800 on the AM dial with call letters KIKK.

The calls we received the next day were varied in nature. Some regular listeners wondered what happened to the old station, some country folks called to find if it was for real or a publicity prank, advertisers called in for explanations, and folks called to place advertising. The feedback was almost a hundred percent positive. The station enjoyed fast growth from the start. We had some live shows, lots of interviews, and set up many weekend remotes on a truck bed in front of a grocery store or car agency. In the retail store remotes, we would often book Billy Mize so we could draw the ladies. Smiley Burnett, also known as Frog Millhouse, was a huge draw for the kids.

In the early 1960's, the station call letters were changed to KUZZ to be a country cousin to the pop stations in town. I first put up an argument that Herb Henson might resent the call letters, and that it might cause some confusion, but Bob Scott was a true radio man and promoter. The call letters were changed overnight. A few months later, upon Scott's departure, Cousin Herb became manager of the station.

Around this time, I took a new Patsy Cline record into a station in Tulare, California, and met a young man named Larry Daniels working there. He was so professional, and he loved his work. He was around twenty years old, but he looked even younger. I asked if I could interest him in an interview at KUZZ. He said yes, kept the interview, was hired and became a top-notch radio personality. Bill Woods always put a moniker on everyone, so Larry was named Shotgun Daniels. There were some great radio personalities along the way, including Larry Scott, nicknamed Boothill Scott, Bill Strength, and many others over the years. When Larry Scott was there, we had a pickup softball team with Scott as the pitcher.

The station continued to do well and grow under Cousin Herb's leadership. Then on November 26, 1963, a short time after completing his "The Trading Post Show" on television, Herb passed away of a heart attack. The city and country music was in shock, even more so because this happened just a few days after the assassination of President Kennedy. Herb, at thirty-eight years of age, was greatly missed. His personality and salesmanship had done great things for country music in the San Joaquin Valley. He had showcased several entertainers that went on to international careers, and made a huge contribution to the birth of the Bakersfield Sound.

In 1966, Buck Owens bought KUZZ radio, and since then, many changes have been made. It is now a 24-hour country music station. KUZZ has won many national awards, and continues to make a great contribution to country music and serves its vast audience with news and entertainment.

I got to know Buck in the early fifties, long before he bought the radio station. In the fall of 1960, I was doing two show a night for the weekend at Doc's Club out on Edison Highway. Just before my first show was over, I looked to my left and saw Buck Owens sit down on a stool in the corner. I didn't think much about it, as several musicians would drop by on occasion, but then he sent word through a waitress that he wanted to talk to me alone. When the first show ended, I went over, and he said quickly, "Don't announce me being here. I wanted to talk to you about working with me. I would like you to become my bandleader. I am taking over the Fresno Barn. That will be my base." He had a couple records at the time, and was just taking off on Capitol. I had known him for a few years, and he had recorded on a couple of my records. I knew how hard he worked, and I was confident he would make it.

He explained that the plan was to book stars to come through and promote crowds enough to raise funds for him to travel to radio stations to promote his records or do interviews and appearances when possible. My job would be to lead the band and keep it going while he was out of town. We talked for a while. He told me about a young guitar and fiddle player named Don Rich, and how he wanted to help develop Don's skills.

He told me to think about it, and we would talk on Monday. I talked it over with my brother, and he agreed to lead the Valley Rhythm Boys while I was away with the Buck Owens Show. I went over to Buck Owens's house on Monday, and we made plans.

The following weekend, we were off and running. Buck's band consisted of Don on guitar, fiddle, and vocals, Bonnie Owens on vocals and back up, Wayne Stone on drums, Lavonia Morrison on vocals and back up, Jay McDonald on steel guitar, and myself playing rhythm, vocals, and doing the announcing. Buck would often play lead guitar with us when he was in town, and we were known then as the Buck Owens Band. Sometime later, Merle Haggard played bass with us and began calling the band the "Buckaroos," and it stuck. During this time, we booked many stars of the day.

Buck was married to Phyllis then. She was so special, a real professional, and a joy to work with. We were able to pay all the bills that came up, with enough for Buck to travel the Northwest and Midwest when necessary. After a while, he was able to find work on television and clubs along the way. As his name grew, he was able to take Don along with him.

Sometimes we would do package shows with several stars, and over the years, I became friends with a number of them. One was an Opry star named George Morgan. I recall him saying one time, "I'm anxious to get home and see my baby daughter Lorrie." Some other friends I made were the Wilburn brothers, Doyle and Teddy, and Don Helms, who was Hank Williams' long time steel player. The three of them were partners in a new publishing venture. I introduced them to a young Johnny Russell, a singer who was learning to write country songs, and I put him on stage for them to hear. They invited him to Nashville where he became a big Opry star, and teamed up later with our girl singer, Lavonia Morrison. Together they wrote "Act Naturally," one of Buck's biggest hit songs. They all won several awards.

I worked with Buck for a little over two years, and by that time, he was well on his way and began to need his band on the road. I would make the shows that were close, but I did not want to travel on the road. During my time with him, I got to work with so many great people, like George Jones, Jimmy Dickens, Merle Travis, Wynn Stewart, and Rose, Cal and Fred Maddox. I also got to know Bobby Bare, Cowboy Copas, Carl Belew, Roger Miller, whom I would always sing "Faded Love" with, just so he could play fiddle, Teddy and Doyle Wilburn, George Morgan, Freddy Hart, Skeets McDonald, Joe and Rose Lee Maphis, the Collins kids, and many others. We were a busy group and every minute was fun. Buck worked hard, and expected as much from the band, so there was no drinking allowed and no smoking on stage. That didn't stop he and I from enjoying our pipes offstage, though.

Around this time, I began finding success with my own songs. I was working with my brother-in-law, Charles "Buster" Beam, who lived in Southern California. He liked country music, and was a hard-nosed salesman who offered a lot of ideas in writing, so we became a team with only a handshake. Buck Owens asked me more than once to write him a song, but by then I had begun writing for Patsy Cline. It was only years later, when he was suffering from health issues, that I wrote a song for Buck called "There's Just the Smallest Chance," which he liked, but was never able to record.

I teamed up with Wynn Steward's band and began making demos for 4 Star Music in Pasadena, California. 4 Star was working with Decca Records at the time, and they had T. Texas Tyler, Carl Belew, and Patsy Cline on their roster. In 1958, T. Texas Tyler recorded our songs "Let the Teardrops Fall" and "Confined" on the 4 Star Label. A short time later, on June 6, 1958, Patsy Cline Recorded "Let the Teardrops Fall" on Decca. The song charted, and we were on our way.

I recall telling Bonnie Owens during a show in Porterville, CA about Patsy's recording of "Let the Teardrops Fall." She was so excited for me that she asked me to write the words down. She called Fuzzy Owen over, and the three of us huddled up in the corner while they learned the melody. They then went on stage with Herb Henson's band from the "Trading Post" show, and though they had never heard the song before, the band played the background music without any rehearsal while Bonnie and Fuzzy sang a duet of "Let the Teardrops Fall." They did a fine job of it, and that performance is a lasting memory for me.

When Cliffie Stone did a radio show live from the Huntington Hotel in Pasadena, he had two girl singers who performed on the show, Jeanie and Janie Black. My writing partner, Buster Beam, and I were friends of the Blacks, and were writing songs for Patsy Cline. With Cliffie's blessing, the girls would sing our songs on the show as a way to preview them. We often attended the radio show and enjoyed the many talents that performed there.

On February 23, 1959, Patsy recorded our song "Yes, I Understand" with a great arrangement. Hank Garland's guitar riff was outstanding. On July 20, 1959, she recorded our song, "I'm Blue Again," and in March 1960, she recorded our song, "How Can I Face Tomorrow." On August 1, 1960, she recorded our song, "Crazy Dreams," her first modern country recording with a shuffle beat. Another of our songs recorded by Patsy was a rockabilly song called "Love, Love Me Honey Do." These songs have reached gold on several albums, and all six were on the Patsy Cline collection album, which went platinum. Many of these songs have been on television series and used in various scenes. "Let the Teardrops Fall" was used on the next to last program of "The Sopranos."

Several of our songs have been recorded by other artists, such as Porter Wagoner's recording of "My Baby's Not Here in Town Tonight," which reached Number 3 on Cashbox. The same song was also recorded by Carl Belew on Decca, Norma Jean on RCA, and a great recording by Rusty Draper on Monument. He used the Nashville Brass with an arrangement like Johnny Cash had on "Ring of Fire." Janie Frickie recorded "Crazy Dreams" on her MCA "Saddle the Wind" album, and had much success with worldwide sales. "Let the Teardrops Fall" was recorded in later years by a rock and roll band in Germany called The Brandos, and they used the same guitar arrangement that Hank Garland used on Patsy's version. Buster and I have been blessed with so many recordings of these songs over the years, and many others were recorded on independent labels.

In 1978, I became a full time publisher and formed Jiles Beam Music. Later, I bought Beam Records from Buster. We recorded Kathy Bee on a tribute album to Patsy Cline with twelve songs, and a Christmas album called "Legend of the Tabby Cat," which was well received. A recent gospel recording by Luanne Hunt on American Classic Recordings of my song "I Want to Stand Where Jesus Stood," which appeared on several playlists around the world, was on the ballot for a Grammy nomination in 2009. We did not win, but, as they say, being on the ballot was something. Other girls who had a lot of success with "Let the Teardrops Fall" are Kathy Robertson and Jann Browne.

Altogether, I was lucky enough to have songs on eight gold albums and six songs on Patsy Cline's platinum album. I have enjoyed success with writing and performing music, but if I can claim any credit for the birth of the Bakersfield Sound, it was in the help I gave to Buck Owens, and in my contribution to the founding of the radio station KUZZ.

In 1996, Buck presented me with one of his famous red, white, and blue guitars. The engraving on the pick guard reads, "To Lawton Jiles, a friend for forty years. May your mountaintops be many and your waterloos be few. Your Pal, Buck Owens. Sept. 6, 1996." It hangs proudly in my studio in Upland, California, and draws much attention. He also wrote a nice letter that hangs beside the guitar.

Over the years, Buck and I reminisced about the creation of the Bakersfield Sound. I also spoke with Bonnie Owens about it, and all of us agreed that there were no plans or concerted efforts to bring about the creation of the Sound. No one realized we were watching country music being reinvented. Everyone just wanted to play good music and please the crowd.

I am now a proud charter member of the Bakersfield Country Music Museum, with an exhibit of memorabilia items on display there. I perform there often to help raise funds for the museum and enjoy the friendship of many old friends still around. So many of them are gone now, but the BCMM helps keep their memory and their contributions alive.

Afterword: Buster Beam's Death

It is with deep sadness that I report here the passing of Charles "Buster" Beam on September 20, 2011. He was my writing partner and best friend for fifty years. I will truly miss him.

THE WARRIOR—TOMMY HAYS

Tommy Auery Hays was born October 3, 1929 in Hartshorn, Oklahoma to Benjamin H. and Elizabeth Ann Hays. Tommy was number nine of eleven children, and his father was a coal miner. When Tommy was seven, the family moved to Powhatan, Alabama, a small coal mining town. Tommy says, "There we had electricity but no running water. The water smelled like rotten eggs, but was really cool because it was drawn from the well."

Tommy learned early on how to make money. He enjoyed having ice cream and a coke now and then, and wanted to buy his own. When he was eight, he went around and asked miner's wives if he could sell them small wood for starting morning fires. Tommy began delivering newspapers, and he worked at the miner's bathhouse where the miners would wash up before going home. He would carry water for heating.

When Tommy was twelve, the family moved to Pascagoula, Mississippi during World War II. His father worked in the shipyard. Tommy says, "This probably kept me out of the coal mines."

The family created their own entertainment. Tommy first had a harmonica, then got his first guitar at age ten. His younger brother Kenny got a fiddle, and the two would play at church. In Pascagoula, at age fourteen, Tommy began working at The Pixley Theatre selling popcorn and candy. After a while, he moved up to chief projectionist. It was there that he heard beautiful western music. Looking through the peephole, he learned it was the Sons of the Pioneers, and one of them was playing an electric guitar. Right then, he was hooked and had to learn to play lead.

Tommy grew up fast, married young, and started a family. In 1947, he moved his family to Bakersfield and secured a job at the Granada Theatre as a projectionist. Just around the corner from the theatre was Seth Jayn's Music Store. He made a small purchase there, and they asked him about his playing and ended up hiring him as a teacher. Tommy told them, "I don't read music." They assured him, "Just stay a lesson ahead of your students, and you will be fine." He taught some of the future pickers of Bakersfield.

The music scene in Bakersfield was going well after World War II. Tommy filled in here and there, but always kept himself in some outside enterprise. He liked sales and began working with State Farm Insurance Co. The company was flexible with him during times when he needed to work with his music. Tommy retired from State Farm Insurance after 33 years.

Tommy had an opportunity to play in Las Vegas that first year, alongside Anita Cross, her husband, and a drummer that would later work for me in the fifties and in the sixties with Buck Owens. His name was Mel King.

In 1948, Tommy formed a band called Tommy Hays and the Western Swingsters. Sixty years later, they still perform under the same name. They began work at the Beardsley Ballroom with a nine-piece band. He also did an afternoon show on KMPC radio advertising the Saturday night dance at Beardsley, the showplace for artists appearing in Bakersfield during this time. Tommy's band would often back them or open for these performers, the likes of which included Earnest Tubb, Jimmy Wakely, Jimmy Dickens, Tennessee Ernie Ford, and many others. Some asked him to tour with them, but he was a family man and loved Bakersfield too much. Tommy worked every club in town over the years, starting with The Blackboard Café. He moves on to The Lucky Spot, Clover Club, Rainbow Gardens, The Pumpkin Center Barn, and all of the Edison Highway Clubs. Tommy also ran a moving milk route six days a week during this time.

Tommy worked with Billy Mize and Cliff Crofford on their television show. Early in 1948, he worked with Bob Smith, one of the early pioneers doing theatre shows.

Tommy has always been community minded, giving his time and efforts to various fundraisers. He has been a member of the Kern County mounted sheriff's posse for years, raising funds for children's programs. Tommy is a lifetime member of the Bakersfield County Music Museum, serving as advisor and performing with his band for various fundraisers.

Tommy's contribution to the birth of the Sound has no limit. He promoted shows and helped to keep the public support that gave the performers the opportunity to develop their talents. Without musicians like Tommy Hays, there may never have been a sound so recognized around the world.

MR. FOCUS—LARRY PETREE

Larry Petree was born in Oklahoma, and his family migrated to California in 1941. He became a Bob Wills fan while still in high school and fell in love with the steel guitar. He especially loved the style of Herb Ramington, and would catch their show each time Bob Wills came to town. He worked and saved and finally earned enough money to buy a steel guitar of his own. He took some lessons, then heard a young man whose sound was much like Herb Remington's sound. That young man's name was Billy Mize.

Larry took some lessons from Mize, but when Larry was drafted into the Korean War, the lessons stopped. When he was discharged, Larry's interest had not faded, but Billy was into his career now and could not give him full-time lessons. So Larry looked for help anywhere he could.

In 1953, I met Larry at a jam session at a club called The Blue Moon Café in Richgrove, California, soon to change its name to The Lucky Club. My brother and I had a band called The Valley Rhythm Boys. I had not been out of the service for very long, and we were trying to regroup, so Larry joined our band. Larry liked swing music and loved the Hank Thompson sound. He could draw on the Brazo Valley Boys driving sound, which added a lot to our dance band.

Hank Thompson was very popular and had a top honky-tonk sound, so we worked on some of his arrangements, especially after Billy Garner joined us on lead guitar. Now we had a six-piece swing band that could do the job: Larry on steel guitar, Billy Garner on lead, Del Baker on piano and fiddle, my brother Johnny on bass, myself on guitar, emcee, and vocals, and often, Dean Trammel on fiddle to give us a twin fiddle sound.

Larry was very involved in arrangements and very serious about his music, always striving for perfection. He spent close to six years with the Valley Rhythm Boys, and over the years, he worked with most of the musicians in Bakersfield music. He has recorded with most of them and played backup for many country stars. Hank Thompson loved his playing and offered Larry a touring job with him. Larry did not accept the offer but has played many shows with Thompson when he was in the Bakersfield area.

Larry worked on the Jimmy Thompson television show, and even played a part in a network television movie filmed in Taft, California. Larry was part of the group as a consultant with Jimmy Addington and others that formed the Bakersfield Country Music Museum, and he worked hard selling memberships. Larry is a charter member of the museum and plays with the bands that appear at the events. He can claim his share of credit for his long time support of the Bakersfield Sound. Some of his exhibits can be found at the museum.

THE BARBERSHOP DRUMMER—
JIMMY PHILLIPS

Jimmy Phillips is one of the few homegrown Bakersfield musicians. Jimmy was born in 1941, in a town just outside of Bakersfield called Weedpatch. Jimmy began playing the drums in the third grade and continued all through high school. At age fifteen, he played throughout Southern California with a popular hometown rock band called the Jolly Jody and the Go Daddys.

In the early sixties, at the age of nineteen, Jimmy began his country career just like everyone else. He went to work for Bill Woods. He also worked the Thomason television show. He recorded with many stars of the day with RCA, Capitol, and Tower Records. He worked with such stars as Barbara Mandrell, Merle Haggard, Freddy Hart, and Glen Campbell. He also worked some with Buck Owens and The Buckeroos, and did a stint with Waylon Jennings in Las Vegas. Jimmy was a vocalist and drummer in the Shot Gun Daniels Band, and currently records gospel music on his own label.

Jimmy lives in Tehachapi, California with his wife Diane where they own a barbershop. Diane is an artist, and her work is displayed in their business. Their walls are filled Diane's art, music memorabilia, and of course mirrors, so the customers can see themselves. Many pictures on display are related to the Bakersfield Sound, Jimmy's career, and his many friends. Jimmy became a barber when he finished high school and has maintained his license ever since, much like Perry Como did.

Jimmy has done much to support country music and the Bakersfield Sound. He and his wife Diane are very much a part of the Bakersfield Country Music Museum. Diane has served on the board for some time with Jimmy as a supporter and consultant.

MR. RHYTHM—HENRY SHARPE (AKA HENRY SHOPSHIRE)

Henry was born in Eufoula, Oklahoma in McIntosh country to Henry J & Eva Mae Shopshire. He had ten brothers and sisters. It was a beautiful part of Oklahoma with a gorgeous lake and lots of timber. Henry was always interested in music, even as a young boy.

As he grew older, he would sit in with locals to sing and sometimes play drums. In 1950, Chuck Harding and The Colorado Cow Hands were playing in McCalister, Oklahoma, and Henry sang a couple of songs with them. Chuck went on back to Missouri, and a short time later, he called Henry and asked him if he wanted a job. Henry said, "Well, maybe, but I don't play solos!"

Chuck said, "Good." Henry worked with him for six years.

Henry kept hearing about the movement in music going on in Bakersfield. He and his wife Margaret Ann loaded up the car and made the move to Bakersfield, where he did odd jobs and sat in with different bands, getting to know the local musicians. He liked the Blackboard Café, so when Johnny Cuviello left, Bill Woods called Henry and asked, "Do you want this job?"

Henry said, "Who's calling?"

When Bill identified himself, Henry insisted, "I don't do solos!"

Bill told him, "Good." Henry began at the Blackboard in 1958, often working seven days a week and doing two shows, a radio show and the Sunday night show, on Sunday.

Henry worked with Buck Owens, who played lead guitar, Bill Woods on guitar and sometimes steel, Lawrence Williams on piano, and Don Markham on trumpet and saxophone, with Henry himself on drums and vocals. He also filled in on local television shows. Henry worked at the Blackboard for five years and nine months during a time when the birth of the Bakersfield Sound was in full bloom.

A lot of recordings were being made in Hollywood, and Henry was part of that, too. Rose Maddox always loved to work with Henry, even though she was usually rough on drummers. Henry backed many stars of the day that appeared at the Blackboard during a time when it may have been the best-known country music nightclub in the country. The stars all loved the Blackboard and the lively dance crowds. The drums were located off to the side of the bandstand, so the fans would often give their request to the drummer, which was Henry. Buck and Merle were also there in 1962, and at that time, neither one wanted to sing because they only wanted to play guitar. Henry said his biggest job was getting them to sing because the requests proved that everyone wanted to hear them.

Henry's solid beat, and his efforts in keeping the crowds happy and give the singers a chance to develop their talents certainly made him a big part of the birth of the Bakersfield Sound. He and Cuviello both were so important to the hard-driving, honky-tonk sound that was so integral to the Bakersfield Sound.

Henry was on the founding committee that helped form the Bakersfield Country Music Museum (BCMM). His hard work and dedication in the early going was inspirational and so helpful in getting the idea off the ground. Henry passed away on March 10, 1998 and his energy, talent, and personality are truly missed by all who had the pleasure of knowing him.

MR. EVERYDAY—
JELLY SANDERS

Jelly Sanders was a transplanted Okie born in Duncan, Oklahoma. His family migrated to Porterville in 1938 in the height of the Great Depression. He began playing music as a teenager, and worked the nightclubs on the weekends while doing day jobs as well. Jelly was a cousin of Bob Wills, so if Bob was in the area, Jelly would often set in with the band.

Jelly had a band in the late forties called The Rhythm Rangers. They played a lot of Western swing music, Bob Wills style. He operated out of the Porterville Sports Center, where Maddox and Rose held court and other artists of the day would appear. Jelly worked some with Jean Sheppard and Ferlin Huskey.

In the early fifties, Jelly joined the Cousin Herb television show in Bakersfield, and had his own TV show for a while after Herb's passing.

Jelly was a master on the fiddle. He also played acoustic guitar, electric guitar, and bass. He was a good vocalist, so he was always in demand as a musician and as a recording artist. He recorded with so many folks other than Bakersfield artists, and was on most of Buck

Owens' early releases. Jelly played the same fiddle that he began playing on when he was six years old.

Jelly passed away August 20, 1996, and Bakersfield lost a true warrior. His contribution to the birth of the Bakersfield Sound was monumental. He was influential as a teacher, and besides being a first-rate musician, he was also a very loyal friend and was always accountable. Bakersfield fans still have fond memories of Jelly Sanders. His son Jimmy carries on the family tradition.

THE DOCTOR—GENE MOLES

Oklahoma born, Denver Eugene Moles Sr. grew up in the San Joaquin Valley. In the mid-thirties, his family moved to Selma, an area where you could hear plenty of country music stations and many live shows, such as Maddox Brothers and Rose, each morning He began playing guitar at age 15 and never looked back.

Gene joined Tex Butler in Bakersfield and played for a short while at the Blackboard Café. He played with many other bands and in many clubs in town, and he joined the Jimmy Thomason television show in the early fifties. One of his achievements was playing on Buck Owens' first session for Capitol Records.

Gene always enjoyed playing jazz with Don Rich. He honed his guitar licks in the early stages of rock 'n' roll. He spent several years with Semi Mosely, building guitars and serving as quality control director. Gene played on many recordings for Bakersfield musicians and played on many hit recordings for Red Simpson, one of which was "Highway Patrol." The song later became a great hit when it was recorded by Junior Brown, and was featured on the movie soundtrack using the same arrangement Gene had on the original recording.

Gene was always ready to fill in and help when called upon. Cousin Herb used him often. Gene had many offers to move to Nashville and become a studio musician, but he never wanted to leave Bakersfield. His son, Gene Moles Jr., is a Nashville musician and has been there for some time.

For years, Gene operated his own guitar shop in east Bakersfield where he repaired guitars. He became known as the "Guitar Doctor." He also could, and did, build some guitars on his own. He was a solid, unselfish guitar player. I shared the stage several times with Gene and was always happy to work with him. He had the hard-driving sound so important to the Bakersfield Sound, but could play a tender ballad with as much feeling as anyone.

In 1961, Gene met Nokie Edwards of the Ventures, and co-wrote three songs of the surf rock sound popular at the time. They songs were titled "Sunny River," "Night Run," and "Scratch."

Gene passed away from lung disease at the age of seventy-three on April 28. He is survived by his wife of forty-six years, Joan, and four children. Gene's contributions to the birth of the Bakersfield Sound were numerous. He played on many of the early recordings with a sound that was similar to Roy Nichols' and Don Rich's. They often played together. Gene's influence was great, and some of his work was duplicated by others almost note for note. Musicians and fans will long remember Gene, his gentle ways, and great talent.

THE SIDEMEN

The recording of "A Dear John Letter" in 1953 put the "can do" in the Bakersfield musicians' vocabulary. All of the musicians and sidemen took note.

In 1954, Bud Hobbs, a local recording artist with MGM Records, was working some with Bill Woods. I used to run into him at the Blackboard Café. He could really put on a show with the "Truck Drivin' Man." They worked up an arrangement on a tune called "The Louisiana Swing." The sidemen were Buck Owens on lead guitar, Oscar Whittington and Jelly Sanders on twin fiddles, and Bill Woods on piano. This song was recorded with a honky-tonk attitude and sounded very much like what later would be called the Bakersfield Sound. These musicians would lead the way on future recordings. When musicians like Roy Nichols came to town, he added more focus to what was already there. Buck handed down his raw, in-your-face telecaster sound to Don Rich. Other guitar men followed in their footsteps.

Oscar Whittington was there from the beginning. He was a boyhood friend of Bill Woods, and was always available for any job needed. He was a member of Ferlin Husky's band called The Termites.

Jelly Sanders was an all-around musician, a great fiddle player who could play lead guitar, acoustic guitar, and sing. Jelly did a lot for television and was in constant demand as a recording musician as well. He did many recordings with Buck Owens, Merle Haggard, Red Simpson, and others.

Bill Woods was all things and played on many records for many artists besides Bakersfield artists.

Before reaching stardom himself, Buck Owens recorded with many artists. Artists like the great Tommy Hays, there from the beginning, played a huge part in the support of Bakersfield artists, along with his brother Kenny.

Fuzzy Owen, steel guitarist and vocalist, played on many records, and became a producer along with his cousin Lewis Talley. Fuzzy has managed Merle Haggard from the start of Merle's career.

Gene Moles, lead guitarist, appeared on many records, displaying his talent on Red Simpson sessions and many others.

Billy Mize, although a recording artist himself, was a great steel player and played on many sessions for other artists.

Johnny Cuviello, a former Bob Wills drummer, who was still playing like a 20-year-old at the age of 90, was always ready to step in when called upon.

A special tribute is owed to Tom Brumley, steel guitar player with the Buckaroos for many years. Tom continued the Sound on Buck's recordings that had Ralph Mooney's stamp throughout. Ralph was followed by Jay McDonald, then JD Maness filled in for a while before Tom became a fixture and put his stamp on the Sound, as can be heard in "It's Crying Time." Tom passed away in San Antonio, Texas on February 3, 2009. He was the son of gospel composer Albert E. Brumley.

Doyle Holly was a sideman for a while before joining Buck Owens and the Buckaroos for several years, playing bass on many of Buck's hit records. Doyle later became a recording artist in his own right, with Top 10 results.

Don Markham honed his craft at the Blackboard, learning to play the sax and the trumpet in the country keys G, A, D and E, unusual keys for a horn player. Bill Woods gave Don the stage and he made the most of it. Since 1980, Don has been a big part of Merle Haggard's band as a musician and backup singer.

Bobby Galardo was a drummer who worked on many records and countless demos. He was part of The Strangers in the '80s, along with Biff Adams, a drummer who has also recorded many sessions with Merle.

Henry Sharp was a drummer and one of the favorites of Rose Maddox. He played on many sessions at Capitol for Rose and other artists, and was a fixture at the Blackboard for many years. Henry was also one of the organizers of the Bakersfield Country Music Museum (BCMM).

Joe and RoseLee Maphis were big contributors to the popularity of Bakersfield music. They were part of the "Town Hall Party" and worked alongside Billy Mize and Cliff Crofford. They made many appearances in Bakersfield and even moved to Bakersfield for a while, working with Cousin Herb on "The Trading Post Show" and doing shows at the Blackboard Café. Joe wrote a song after one show called "Dim Lights, Thick Smoke, and Loud, Loud Music," and it became an anthem for the Blackboard Café.

Other Bakersfield musicians who were helpful and supportive include guys like Jack Collier, Sonny O'Brien, Gene Oldham, Jimmy Tapp, Jay Goddard, Jimmy Phillips, and Bill Vibe. Others include James Garner, Noble Garner, Toby Minter, Mel King, Billy Garner, and Kenny Pressley, who played the drums on Buck Owens' recording of "Act Naturally." Sadly, Kenny lost his life in an auto accident shortly after returning to Bakersfield at the end of a tour.

Lloyd Green, a blind guitar and fiddle player, worked with Bill Woods early on at the Clover Club. Bill said, "He played the 'Orange Blossom Special' better than anyone I ever heard play it." That's where Bill chose the band's name, the Orange Blossom Playboys.

Some of the early musicians were Cousin Eb Pilling, Tex and Frank Marshall, Jimmy Jeffries, Kenny Hays, Tex Butler, Jack Trent, Bob Smith, Don Savage and his wife Inez Savage, a long-time board member with the Bakersfield Country Music Museum. Other early musicians include Buster Simpson, Dean Trammel, Larry Petree, Del Baker, Bill Muse, Dude Wheeler, Eddie Clark, Johnny McAtee, George French, and Leo Eiffert, who worked in Bakersfield with Billy Garner in the late sixties. Still more musicians deserve to be named, such as Jimmy Bankston, Kurt Webb, Mark Shannon, Jim Bob Sedgwick, Ray Heath, Lawrence

Williams, Odel Johnson and his son, Sonny, Gene McGraudy, Waylan Paget, and Johnny Jiles.

These sidemen, and many others not mentioned here, were very instrumental in the birth of the Bakersfield Sound. They helped hold the crowds in the clubs and on television, and they gave the artists a forum in which to develop their craft and fan base. Without their contribution, the birth of the Bakersfield Sound would not have been what it was.

THE CLUBS

The mother club of Bakersfield was the Blackboard Café, owned by Frank Zabaleta and Joe Limi. Both were steady hands, and their understanding of the club business allowed them to become leaders of the nightclubs in Bakersfield. They would book some of the biggest stars in country music, from local talent to Grand Ole Opry stars, and they could always draw a crowd, even midweek. They also did a live radio broadcast jam session every Sunday afternoon. Bill Woods was the bandleader and the headliner there for 16 years. A lot of the Bakersfield recording stars started out there, like Buck Owens, Merle Haggard, Tommy Collins, Billy Mize, Fuzzy Owen, Lewis Talley, and Cliff Crofford.

The second club was the Luck Spot in east Bakersfield on Edison Highway, owned by Bob Warner. The Lucky Spot was a very popular dance club and always had great bands with good dance music. They did not feature guest stars there, as they had their own. Billy Mize was there for years, and Cliff Crofford, Johnny Barnett, Jelly Sanders, and even Merle Haggard worked there for a while. Fuzzy Owen, Roy Nichols, Lewis Talley, Gene Moles, and Gene McGraudy also all worked there.

The Clover Club was owned by Therman Billings. It was also a hot spot for good music and dancing. All of the local musicians worked there at one time or another, going back to the late forties. This is where a young Bonnie Owens had her first experience as a cocktail waitress and a singer. Fuzzy Owen and Lewis Talley were there when Cousin Herb Henson hired the Clover Club Band to work his television show in the early fifties.

Another early club was Trouts in Oildale, the oldest honky-tonk club in town. Trouts was opened by Ralph Trout in 1945 at the end of WWII. It is still going strong, and is now operated by T. Rockwell. Many old-timers still enjoy a good dance there too.

Some other early clubs going in the forties and fifties were the Rhythm Rancho, the Sad Sack, the Pump Room, Doc's Club, The Green Door, Foster Wards, and High Pockets, where Merle Haggard got his start. There was also the Blue Moon Café in Richgrove, Paul's Cocktail Lounge in Tehachapi, Dick McNutt's Cellar Club in Delano, and The Cuckoo Inn, where Del Reeves started out and Jerry Hobbs worked for a while.

There were other small clubs that would offer live music on the weekends. Tex's Barrel House, owned by Tex Franklin, followed the closing of the Blackboard Café in the late sixties. Bill Woods worked there for a while after the closing of the Blackboard Café. The club scene changed after several of the folks we have written about in this book moved on to the national stage. Some of the club owners retired, and The Lucky

Spot burned. The Blackboard Café and the Palomino closed. More television stations and the popularity of videos made home entertainment more enjoyable. Law enforcement also became stricter with the nightclubs in California, and lawsuits became more common. Club owners did not want the risk or the high cost of insurance.

THE REAL STARS

The inspiration, the need, and the support for the birth of the Bakersfield Sound could be placed with the dance crowd in Bakersfield, or with dancers in all of California, for that matter. They were as near to professionals as you could find. They would come early, stay late, and dance the night away. They were the critics of the band, the music they played, and they were the true test of a band's success.

Perhaps that explains why there were so few of the chosen ones who worked these bands. All totaled, probably less than forty-five musicians worked the clubs over two or three decades. These were dedicated musicians who knew from experience how to please and hold a crowd. There were sidemen who could fill a spot for a relief, but even they had to be very special to enter this crowd as a regular.

These musicians, along with the nightclubs, the dedicated owners, and the dance crowds, were all a necessary part of the birth of the Bakersfield Sound. When listening to a Bakersfield writer's song, a person feels their foot move, whether because of the lyrics, the lead instrument, or perhaps some combination of the two.

In 1959, the Valley Rhythm Boys were playing a special barn dance in a real barn in Porterville, California. We were surprised and very pleased when several dancers came up to be with us, all from the Lawrence Welk crowd who drove through the driving rain from Santa Monica, California.

Entertainers like Bill Woods, Buck Owens, Bill Mize, and others knew how to please their dancers and keep them dancing till closing time. Some of the folks from the dance crowds are still around and come out to Trouts for the Bakersfield Country Music Museum fundraisers. Some of them first met in these clubs, and some request songs that were their favorites at that time. Some still dance to almost every tune that is played. When guys like Red Simpson and Tommy Hays are on stage, they still recognize some of the licks from the past.

In the eighties and nineties, radio was once again filled with Bakersfield guitar licks and vocal sounds. Merle Haggard and Buck Owens' influence could be heard throughout country music. Bakersfield still has a lot of the Sound there, even though most of the clubs are gone. Trouts is the oldest and still going strong. Buck's Crystal Palace is perhaps the main showcase now, with Buck's son Buddy carrying on the family tradition.

Los Angeles, "the town south of Bakersfield," has several musicians who play with a honky-tonk attitude, such as Cody Bryant on guitar, fiddle, and banjo; Rick Shea on lead guitar, mandolin, and steel; Doug Livingston on steel guitar and piano; and Brantly Kearns on fiddle and mandolin. I cannot fail to also mention Mike Stone on guitar, Brian Chapman on bass, Steve Kuhn on drums, Joe Eiffert and his father Leo Eiffert, J.D. Maness, and Al Bruno. Many others still continue to play these sounds.

I enjoy watching the "Marty Stewart Show" on the RFD channel. It reminds me of the Buck Owens Band we had at the Fresno Barn in the early sixties with the honky-tonk attitude and the happy spirit they display on the show. The five-piece band, all smiles and energy, shares everything with its audience. It sounds like and feels like the band we had back then with Don Rich and Buck on guitars, Wayne Stone on drums, Jay McDonald on steel, Bonnie Owens and Voni Morrison on vocals, and me on rhythm. I listen and enjoy with a happy heart. I feel blessed to have been a part of it all and to have shared some historical times, even though I had no idea at the time this was part of the birth of the Bakersfield Sound.

GETTING THE WORD OUT—RADIO

Radio stations in the forties and fifties were very good about working with country music, live programs, recorded shows, and DJ programs years before a full-time country station came on the air. Some of the people we have written about in other chapters had a part in radio, some for 15-minute shows, some for 30-minute shows, and always long enough to promote the shows or clubs where they were working. Folks like Bill Woods, Cousin Herb Henson, Billy Mize, Cliff Crofford, Jimmy Thomason, Thad Buckley, Ferlin Husky, myself, and others spent time on the air either spinning or playing live country music.

Country came along years before KUZZ Radio, which is now a 24-hour station. The radio stations of the day were KAFY, KGEE, KPMC, and KBIS in Bakersfield, KCHJ in Delano, KDRU in Dinuba, KFI and KVFD in the Los Angeles area, KCSB in San Bernardino, KBUC in Corona, KXLA in Pasadena, and KFOX in Long Beach. These stations and others in the valley and along the coast were always supportive and provided a power base for the musicians to build upon. The stations and their DJs were all a vital part of the birth of the Bakersfield Sound.

THE GOOD NEIGHBOR—
THE TOWN SOUTH OF
BAKERSFIELD

The completion of a freeway over the mountain connecting Bakersfield and Los Angeles played a big part in the growth of country music in the fifties. The Bakersfield musicians could travel to Los Angeles and Hollywood for recording sessions and still be able to return to Bakersfield for their television shows and nightclub appearances. The same was true for Los Angeles-area country stars who could now find work and still enjoy appearing on the Cousin Herb television program to promote their shows and records.

Los Angeles radio stations were very supportive of the Bakersfield artists. In the forties, fifties, and sixties, many Los Angeles area stations had country DJs playing country music. KXLA in Pasadena, KFOX in Long Beach and KLAC in Los Angeles were all full time country music stations. There were others throughout the area and some out in the Inland Empire, such as KWOW in Pomona. The Los Angeles-area radio stations had a wide broadcast area, and that helped to spread the popularity of Bakersfield music.

The popularity of Bakersfield music was also spread by the television shows like "The Town Hall Party" in Compton and Cliffie Stone's "Hometown Jamboree" in El Monte. These shows were so very important to the birth of the Bakersfield Sound.

The Los Angeles record companies also were supportive of the Bakersfield artists, and found that their honky-tonk attitude could really sell a product. Record sales were always brisk in the Los Angeles market.

The artists in Bakersfield spent a lot of time in the town south of Bakersfield, and always had total respect for their support. Los Angeles and the surrounding areas played an important role and can claim a share in the birth of the Bakersfield Sound for its contributions.

Many thanks go to the record companies, studios, musicians, producers, radio stations, and numerous clubs that booked the artists. Most of all, thank you to the fans and dancers who followed and supported country music.

CPSIA information can be obtained
at www.ICGtesting.com
Printed in the USA
FSHW020902151219
65107FS